D0459510

D. V. Segre

The
High Road
and the
Low

A Study in
Legitimacy, Authority
and
Technical Aid

Allen Lane

To Joseph Agassi

Contents

Preface ix

1 The Setting of the Problem 1

2 Theories and Practices of Aid-to-Development
  since the Second World War 8

3 Micro-Cooperation versus Macro-Cooperation 40

4 Micro-Cooperation Ancient and Modern 67

5 The Israeli Experience 101

Conclusion 144

Appendix 149

Notes 155

Index 173

Preface

The burden of this book is: How to improve technical aid. The obstacles considered most problematic are lack of capital, appropriate techniques and specialized personnel, and especially misunderstandings between donor and recipient. Indeed, it is the misunderstandings which amplify the other obstacles, since with understanding all obstacles may at least be tackled, but not without it.

This book contains five chapters. The first sets out the problem; the second reviews the situation; the third suggests some ways of making the work of the people acting between donor and recipient more efficient; the fourth exemplifies the role of 'the man-in-the-middle' who carries the innovations, on the basis of a number of case histories drawn from the past; the fifth elaborates on the same theme, with reference to the present, and on the basis of the Israeli experience in technical aid.

This plan has been chosen in order to underline one specific aspect of the technical aid system, namely the activation of the recipients' traditional élite to promote some imitation of the imported innovations. This activation seems to me the most important element in all aid-to-development programmes, since any innovation which is not freely internalized and followed sooner or later becomes an imposition which is, and should be, rejected by the social body.

I wish to acknowledge my debt to many people who generously helped me with the conception, writing and correction of this book and contributed to putting into shape the confused ideas which I developed during my years of field work and operational experience.

I am particularly indebted to Mr Eitan Israely, Assistant Director-General of the Israeli Ministry of Agriculture, who opened to me the doors of both understanding and knowledge of what he had done in the field of technical aid. In this matter, Dr Yitzchak Abt, Assistant Director of the Center of Agricultural Cooperation with Developing Countries, Mr Shimon Amir, Assistant Director-General of the Ministry for Foreign Affairs' Department of Technical Cooperation, Israel, and their staffs, provided much useful information.

Professor Max Gluckman, Professor Marc Karp, Dr Yehuda Elkana, Mr Gideon Weigert, and General Shlomo Gazit, Coordinator of Military Government Administration in Occupied Areas, read an earlier draft of the manuscript and offered many useful suggestions for improvement. Dr Michael Saltman of the Department of Anthropology at Haifa University, helped me to implement these suggestions and I should mention in particular his contribution to Chapter 4.

I am also indebted to Professor Joseph Agassi, who painstakingly went over all the drafts of this book and to Mr Edward Luttwak without whose help and encouragement this work would never have been written.

I also feel indebted to the Van Leer Jerusalem Foundation for generously supporting the research and secretarial work involved in preparing the book, the technical burden of which fell on Mrs Devorah Bar-Zemer, who patiently typed and retyped the manuscript, struggling hard with my ignorance of the English language.

Jerusalem, March 1972.

Chapter 1

The Setting of the Problem

To write about aid to developing countries in 1970 is perhaps less fashionable than it was in 1950 or 1960. Then, the illusion of progress through aid, given by the rich to the poor, by the old colonialist nations to the new, independent ones, still seemed to many like one of those Christmas Day rituals when masters put on aprons and, for the duration of the meal, became the servant of their servants. The illusion has lasted longer than the meal, and so, in all probability, will the disillusionment.

I feel, nevertheless, that this is the proper time to write, before the next surge of goodwill catches the limelight. For when the action is swinging there is little opportunity to analyse past failures and take steps to avoid their repetition.

The failures and frustrations of foreign aid hitherto are fairly obvious: it is their causes and the means by which they can be avoided which require some reflection.

Some official documents, for instance the Pearson Report on International Development,[1] deplore the fact that international aid to developing countries, which amounted to eight billion dollars in 1961 and reached twelve billion by 1968, is shrinking at the precise moment when many backward economies are moving rapidly forward, often thanks to their own efforts. But even in these 'developing countries' one is witness to a spirit of disenchantment and of growing wariness, due to many causes, such as the misconceptions and unrealistic expectations on both sides of 'instant development'; the entanglement of aid with political and military liabilities; the desire on the part of the donors to achieve short-term political strategic or economic aims, irrespective of long-term development needs on the part of the recipient; the increasing complexity and seriousness of domestic problems in the developed countries; the misconceptions of development processes in the underdeveloped states, which often see development as a simple continuation of a political struggle for independence.

The one advantage of this sad disillusionment has been its forcing on both 'Partners in Development' some reappraisal of the whole question of bilateral, multilateral, and self-aid-to-development. As a consequence a lot of useful research work has been done, much indispensable information collected, as shown in the many studies commissioned to publicize the results of international cooperation at the end of the first 'Decade of Development'. The best known, apart from the Pearson Report, to which I shall refer often in this volume, are the Jackson Report,[2] the Peterson Report,[3] the Tinbergen Report,[4] the Hannah Report,[5] the Rockefeller Report[6] and the Perkins Report.[7] On the whole, these commissioned inquiries sound like diplomatically phrased collections of directives from politicians to generals at war against underdevelopment, who think that soldiers, given proper drill, uniforms, officers, communications, transport, weapons and ammunition, are able to translate strategy into action. The trouble with war is that, although any fighting unit can be put on parade, not every unit paraded – even if fully equipped – can fight. At least, not hard enough when it faces an enemy which, as in the case of underdevelopment, is a combination of environmental and physical obstacles, collective social and psychological inertia.

The present volume is mainly concerned with efforts to find out why the war waged by the developed countries against the conditions in the non-developed world is going wrong. It does not ask 'Why aid?' Aid has become, for better or for worse, an integral part of modern international relations and – as with charity – it is impossible to distinguish between what the donor does for his own sake and what he does for the recipient's sake. And so it should continue.

As in any war, it is not the quantity of means which counts, but the effectiveness of the way they are used. This is a point which has been recognized by all planners of aid programmes, especially since the multiplier theory has become commonplace among economists. The Pearson Commission, for instance, makes it a central issue in its recommendation calling for redirection of technical assistance. It indicates that the steady and beneficial growth in the percentage of funds used for technical assistance has been unfortunately upset by the increase in the shortcomings in its implementation, with the regrettable net result of a serious impairment of the total value. 'Technical aid,' says the Commission, 'has too often failed to adapt its objectives and methods to the requirements of developing countries – particularly in the fields of agriculture and of education.' 'Above all,' concludes the Commission, 'it has not been adequately integrated with capital assistance.'[8]

The very qualification of assistance as 'technical' alludes to some of the obstacles which it is liable to meet. It is possible to assist an invalid 'technically', by equipping him with an artificial limb. It is harder to assist human beings who are – at least according to their own standards – normal. In the West, people are familiar with the use of 'extended' limbs; for example, with the aid provided by vehicles. But vehicles require roads and drivers. In inexperienced hands, on an unpaved road, they do not necessarily move faster: they offer better chances of breaking the passengers' necks, or of bringing them to a complete standstill.

The misconception implicit in the idea of applying wrong techniques or looking for technical solutions to basically untechnical problems, becomes evident when one reads what the Pearson Report has to suggest for the improvement of 'technical' aid:

Individual technical assistance experts cannot usually be effective without strong institutional support. We recommend that national or international corps of technical assistance personnel should be given adequate career opportunities and that technical assistance work should be encouraged in both the public and the private sector of donor countries.[9]

That, incidentally, is what I mean by 'drivers'.

What would happen if such a recommendation were followed to the letter? It would surely mean the world-wide institutionalization of the careers of international aid officers before their spheres of action were known. It would probably lead to the establishment of parasitic or semi-parasitic organizations, devoting most of their energies and resources to their own bureaucratic existence and development, and having very little time to deal with the problems they are supposed to help solve.

Even if the catastrophic predictions of some experts in the field are exaggerated,[10] there are no grounds for optimism in the future. It has been pointed out that as seventeen rich countries provide aid-to-development to eighty-five poor countries, about 1,000 combinations of bilateral aid or cooperation treaties are open to discussion and revision. This in itself is enough to cast doubt on the possibility of effectively organizing aid in the chaotic political and diplomatic situations in which international cooperation now takes place. The existence of international organizations such as UNESCO, FAO or WHO does not make matters easier. They are not international coordinating bodies, but rather international machineries working on specific lines of their own. Even if their work could be made more efficient, the aim for which they were created forces them to increase their specialization, in a field where a global approach is required.

Development is the result of a simultaneous effort in many sectors. There is no point in developing education, for instance, without at the same time developing agriculture or industry, fields in which education has to be applied. No less important is the fact that the underdeveloped countries represent small economic units, even where their actual territory, as in the case of Sudan, is enormous. In terms of national product, a country like Dahomey is smaller than a provincial European town, and a continent like Africa is less than a European country of the size of Italy. The breaking up of large colonial territories into independent states has, therefore, not contributed to the solution of economic problems. On the contrary, it has contributed to the growth of a nationalistic and separatist spirit – quite understandable in view of their past history – which seems to confine most of them to a situation of micro-states, to mediocrity, stagnation and – with few exceptions – to economic and social regression. The result has been that in spite of the aid distributed to underdeveloped states between 1954 and 1969; in spite of some colossal engineering achievements such as the construction of the Kariba Dam on the Zambesi and the Aswan Dam on the Nile; in spite of the dramatic scientific breakthrough in agriculture which led to what is known as the 'Green Revolution' – in spite of all this, there has been no increase in agricultural production per capita. This, at least, is what we are led to believe by the statistics of the FAO. They show that between 1952 and 1969 the index of per capita production in agriculture remained static at 100 in the Latin American countries, grew to 105 in the Middle East, and fell from 100 to 92 in Africa. In other words, agricultural production has developed exactly parallel with demographic increase and all efforts to develop production have been defeated by the necessity of feeding the new mouths. If the index of per capita agricultural production could be increased by 1 per cent per annum, this would allow Brazil to double the quantity of foodstuff available to her population within 10 years, Egypt within 140 years, and Iraq within $3\frac{1}{2}$ centuries.

Given all this, how can aid be made more effective? Obviously by the realization in both donor and recipient camps that since the key to development is man, there is no point in trying to train him to help himself with methods and techniques which have no relevance to the problems of developing countries and which have, in fact, been copied from countries which achieved their own development a long time ago. After twenty years of aid, there is not yet one organization which has tried to work out a comprehensive system of education for the children of the developing world. Nor does there seem to be any consciousness of the fact that the successful application of methods or techniques of development is dependent not so much on *what* is taught, but mainly on *how, to whom,* and *by whom* it is taught. Thus far, the *how* and *to whom* have been treated as secondary to the *what*. If the *how* were given greater priority, it would be seen that, irrespective of the quantity or nature of aid (the 'hardware' so-called), what ultimately makes aid effective is its ability to help people to help themselves. This is the 'software', that is, the techniques which enable recipients to graft the new modes on to their traditional ones. Let me make my jargon clear: the term software is sometimes used to denote education, techniques, unsubstantial commodities, as opposed to hardware, or the substantial commodities symbolized in the field of aid by the steel mill and the bulldozer. Here I use software to denote intangibles, such as the ability to turn a tribal chieftain into a building contractor.

With this in mind I have tried in Chapter 2 to present the widespread theories of foreign aid. They all relate to hardware, with the possible exception of some later, feeble attempts to introduce some software from the fields of sociology and anthropology.

Chapter 3 is an attempt to formulate in more detail the above contention as an alternative theory of aid.

Chapter 4 contains a few case studies, the major one being a description of the attempts made to westernize and modernize Malagasy society in the nineteenth century. The changes introduced there were the work of a few Europeans, missionaries and adventurers, whose impact on the recipient society was strong because it was amplified by a process of imitation which they activated in the local leadership. Thus, their actions exemplify my theory.

Chapter 5 gives first a brief account of Israeli efforts in technical cooperation with developing countries. The Israeli experience is unique in that it was forced by a shortage of means – both capital and personnel – to develop some substitute for aid of the hardware type. Israel thus developed, by trial and error, socio-economic techniques which were designed to influence the recipient individual rather than his environment. However, the chapter is mainly concerned with the application of the Israeli experience in foreign aid to the development of the agriculture of the occupied territories of the West Bank of the Jordan river. Here, for the first time, a comprehensive model was used to change the environment through changing the habits of the people by activating a process of imitation.

The basic thesis in all five chapters is as follows: development is a process of adaptation of the old to the new. In order to become self-sustaining, it requires a measure of invention which no aid-to-development can offer, since invention (even invention of methods of adaptation of the imported know-how) cannot be copied but must originate from the innate cultural patterns of any civilization. These patterns, as Ruth Benedict noted over thirty years ago,[11] make use 'of a certain segment of the great arc of potential human purposes and motivations . . . just as any culture makes use of certain selected material techniques or cultural traits. Selection is thus the first requirement of any culture because without selection no culture can even achieve intelligibility.' Aid-to-development cannot be just a selection of the techniques which one party transfers to the other. It must also be a selection of the most appropriate segments of 'potential human purposes and motivations', that is, those segments which can best serve as psychological and emotional ground for the techniques of aid-to-development. This second choice can never be made by one side only – donor or recipient: it is the primary task of the man-in-the-middle.

If the subject matter of technical assistance is defined as the transfer of knowledge from one culture to another, it thus becomes a question of human relationships centred round the donor and the recipient. However, this is not a simple two-way relationship. Change is initiated by élites and effected through élites. In terms of contemporary reality, the isolation of an élite that would have been best suited to serve as a carrier of innovation poses a difficult problem. Under colonial rule, change was enforced by a foreign élite. In the contemporary situation, it is effected through the local élite by a process of imitation. What is important here is that the local élite serves as a mediating body through which knowledge is transferred. Consequently, the success in effecting any innovation depends on the status of the élite within the society.

One must also take into account the fact that the transfer of knowledge requires two distinct and often conflicting intellectual and methodological approaches to deal with the problem of bridging cross-cultural differences. One, the relativist approach, deals with the specific problem of translating the conceptual categories of an innovation into the existing frameworks of the conceptual categories of the recipient. The other, the global approach, deals with the entire cross-cultural process of mediation through which change is carried out.

Chapter 2

Theories and Practices of Aid-to-Development since the Second World War

Ever since the Second World War – when foreign aid started to attain substantial dimensions – thinkers, planners, advisers and administrators have all fallen into one or another of two errors concerning the import of modern techniques and techniques of modernization. They have not tried to obtain the legitimation of these by the accepted traditional leadership, assuming that it must be impossible to receive legitimation by an inferior society for superior techniques of foreign origin. They have usually either tried to impose these imported ideas and techniques on the natives, without paying much attention to local traditions or mentality, or they have appealed to local innovators who, though indigenous by birth, are equally foreign in outlook.

Both these concepts of international cooperation crystallized in the optimistic days of the fifties. They were widely affected by the events of the Cold War and by the ideological battle between the contrasting Marxist and free world approaches to the development of former colonial territories. They have produced – at least in the West – many soul-searching analyses of the inadequacies of aid programmes.

Historical development, political competition, and socio-economic feedback of aid on the original ideological motivations of international assistance, can thus be treated as three different phases of the process.

With reference to the history of aid, it should be noted that no complete bibliographical survey exists on international aid and technical assistance to underdeveloped countries. This is hardly surprising, since few subjects have overlapped and ramified into so many other fields of research as that dealing with the problem of aiding the development and integration of 'backward' societies into the modern world.[1] The need to clarify the very meaning of expressions such as 'international cooperation', 'aid', 'assistance', 'technical assistance', has been felt by many authors. From the outset there has been a feeling that some of the confusion in the terminology stemmed from both hypocrisy and hypersentimentality.

Classical assumptions of foreign aid

On the donor side we find that even in unprejudiced reports, such as that prepared by the Pearson Commission on International Development for the National Bank of Reconstruction and Development (p. 136), private investments and private export credits with maturities of longer than one year are listed under 'aid' – a classification which, if taken at its face value, would transform any credit for selling Espresso machines to a developing country into a contribution to development aid.

On the recipient side, there is an ambivalent tendency to stress at one and the same time the right to be helped and the wish to be equal to the donor – an equality which often has to content itself with euphemisms, such as 'cooperation', 'technical assistance', and so on.

The UN Charter makes no specific mention of international assistance. It only speaks of the determination of its members 'to employ international machinery for the promotion of the economic advancement of all peoples'. But the principle of international assistance, in itself, is not new. It appeared in the Dutchman, Grotius, in the seventeenth century, and in the works of outstanding sixteenth-century jurists, such as the Spaniard, Vitoria. They spoke at length of the duty of the metropolitan States towards the less developed territories under their control or protection.[2] What is certainly both new and significant in our time is the passionate search for new words to express old ideas. Although many of the political motivations of aid have not radically changed, modern international assistance has had to be aligned – at least in its terminology – with the pretension of political equality among States, in a world of growing economic and political power disparity.

If the motivation behind aid from the 'haves' to the 'have nots' has not changed much over the past generation, the importance and the techniques of aid have. The language of international cooperation, like the idea of the development of the under-developed, has grown in status since the end of the Second World War. The duty to help 'backward countries or societies' has become the duty to 'cooperate with developing countries', 'backwardness' being left for areas well inside the most developed countries of the world, such as the slums of New York, the 'depressed zones' in the French Jura or Sicily. As a result of the reluctance to apply expressions such as 'backwardness', 'retardation' or 'decay' to new States, the true implication of these words has been transferred to other expressions, such as 'modernization' or 'underdevelopment of the developing', without gaining much clarity or content in the process.

The machinery of aid has also undergone drastic change. Almost every 'donor' government has felt the need to have special ministries or agencies to administer international cooperation; almost every large industrial concern has spent money or supported some office for training the untrained of the Third World; old and new philanthropic and religious societies have developed schemes to help the 'have nots' side by side with some bureaucracy to cope with the problem. Multilateral or international organizations, such as the Common Market and the United Nations agencies, have tended to equate the size of their aid-to-development structures with the immensity of the job they hope to carry out in the distant future, rather than with the unfinished jobs already in hand.

Critique of classical assumptions

Recent United Nations reports, such as the Jackson Report or the Pearson Report, already mentioned, or the works of such economists as Gunnar Myrdal[3] or J. K. Galbraith,[4] have examined the existing aid machinery as well as the motives behind them. They give an almost impressionistic picture of the current dissatisfaction with the organization and the realization of international cooperation.

The Jackson Report, for example, largely consists of criticism of the faulty machinery of UN aid agencies, a presentation of their shortcomings, and some strongly argued proposals for correction. I shall ignore the proposals since they do not concern the major theme of the present volume. Nor am I concerned in this study with the relative weight of the 'machinery' in the United Nations, or of any other aid machinery. It is, however, difficult to disagree with the conclusion drawn by the Jackson Report (p. 14) that the 'machine' has a recognizable identity of its own, and has so much power that the question inevitably arises as to who controls this machine which – in Jackson's view – is becoming 'slower and more unwieldy, like a prehistoric monster'.

Turning from the machine to the motivations behind it, one finds economist Gunnar Myrdal, in his book, significantly called *The Challenge of World Poverty: A World Anti-Poverty Program in Outline*, challenging the self-interested motivations of the donor States and the mainly economic approach to the problems of aid. Such an approach 'abstracts from attitudes and institutions' of the recipient countries (p. 10), and the confusion between economic and non-economic factors among planners of aid. Myrdal also denounces the self-defeating efforts of planners who – mindful of the traditional valuation of the developing countries – seek 'goals for development' in these same traditional valuation efforts, efforts which, for him, amount to 'abstaining from rational planning' (p. 29).

The criticisms of Jackson, Myrdal and Galbraith, among others, contain much truth and one could, without difficulty, bring additional evidence against the motivation and execution of programmes of international cooperation, as practised today by governments and international organizations. The common shortcoming of this type of criticism is that it does not suggest a practical alternative which would enable people engaged in aid to adopt a new attitude to the old problem. For anyone who is not a partisan of radicalism in international aid – a contradiction in terms, since the only radicals in aid can be those who have no (material) aid to give – there is no alternative but to work within the existing, admittedly imperfect, 'machinery' and channels, donor or recipient, of aid. In other words, these critics suggest either doing more or better of what is already being done, or (as Myrdal, among others, suggests in his 'policy conclusions', pp. 363–85) altering the motives of the people involved.

The former argument inevitably clashes with limitations of

funds and specialized manpower; the latter is equally impracticable given the present, highly unsatisfactory, international political set-up. There is little doubt that *if* governments could be induced to renounce the use of force, and *if* a world government could be established in place of a multiplicity of egotistical ones, *then* things might be better for everyone. But this is very unlikely to happen in the foreseeable future. Given the hard facts of the present, what are we to do now?

The answer which this study tries to offer is that, in view of the real shortcomings of modern aid-to-development, it might perhaps be useful, after clarifying why it works so badly, to see if a way exists of producing an operative methodology capable of cranking the existing structures into more effective action, rather than changing them.

Politicization of aid

For most of the donor countries (with the possible exceptions of Sweden and other Scandinavian countries), aid has become a political or diplomatic weapon for the pursuit of political aims. It has, furthermore, been a difficult weapon to handle, because of its low economic profitability, the strong ideological connotations involved, and the social instability which it tends to produce, the latter often running counter to the donor's political aim of stabilizing the recipient.

The problem cuts deep. Should aid be aimed at short-term or long-term results? On the one hand, the political desire to achieve quick results – sometimes only to satisfy the caprice of a local ruler – has often led to negative results in the medium or long term, which have helped to disqualify foreign assistance in many recipient countries. On the other hand, long-term aid schemes, even if successful, have lost their impact and/or helped to unsettle traditional societies to such an extent that other types of help, for instance military or political, have had to be brought in to keep the existing régime in power. Much of the anti-American political instability in countries like Turkey or Greece, not to speak of Vietnam, seems to be linked to the social instability produced in these areas by American economic aid. In both cases, the politicization of aid has tended to oversimplify many analyses of the complex and often contradictory problems involved in development. The result has been that aid strategists have often reached operational conclusions logical in themselves yet so irrelevant to the solution of the problems of development that they have become a source of much internal quarrelling among influence-seeking people or schools of thought with vested interests in aid.

One such warring trend crystallized in 1957 around the Report to the Senate Committee on 'Objectives of the United States Economic Assistance Program', prepared by MIT's Center of International Studies (and reflecting the ideas expressed elsewhere by two of its most authoritative members, M. Millikan and W. Rostow.[5] This Report suggested that 'comprehensive and sustained' American economic assistance could 'in the short run materially reduce the danger of conflict triggered by aggressive minor powers'.

With remarkable naïveté, many western economists, suddenly transformed into political advisers through the political success of American aid to post-war western Europe, hoped that such assistance would 'help to create the conditions of self-sustained economic growth', which 'in two or three decades' might result 'in an overwhelming preponderance of societies with a successful record of solving their problems without resort to coercion or violence'.[6]

What was surprising in this line of thought was not the faith in economic aid as a lever to self-sustained development (given the experience in European recovery aided by the Marshall Plan), but the belief that poor nations are more aggressive because they are poor. History indicates exactly the contrary. But historical evidence could not shake the faith of positivistic thinkers who, irrespective of their sympathies for liberal or socialist theories, conceived of progress mainly in material terms. They apparently believed that the possession of goods made men less willing to risk them by violence; that leaders conducting their people along the paths of progress are necessarily more moderate, politically speaking, than traditional leaders 'reactionary' enough to maintain the old systems. The cases of 'progressive' Syrian radicalism versus 'feudalist' Kuwait are current examples in the Middle East.

Historical development of economic aid

Historically speaking, the modern idea of mass international aid to underdeveloped countries evolved from the American wartime strategy of using economic aid both as a fighting measure and as a reconstruction system after the fighting had died down. The Marshall Plan was the strategic, economic continuation of the Lend-Lease Act with which the United States sustained Allied military efforts, first against the Axis and later against communism, even before she herself was directly involved in both struggles.

This type of post-war aid was marked by three distinctive features: it was meant to bring about the reconstruction of the economies of highly developed countries ravaged – but by no means wiped out – by the war; it was a multilateral responsibility for the distribution of aid, despite there being one main source of aid; and it emphasized what was considered to be the economic, and subsequently the political crux of the fight – the bridging of the dollar gap between the USA and the European soft currency and sterling areas.

The all-out offensive against the European dollar gap was not only an effort to salvage and galvanize the economies of Europe; it was a practical way of equating the defence of a whole set of ideological, social, cultural and political values, common to the western nations, with the defence of their economic well-being. Financial solvency of European countries was regarded as a powerful ingredient in political and ideological solvency, at least as far as the communist challenge was concerned. The battle for the dollar gap having thus become largely identified with the efforts to achieve the most effective distribution and use of many billions of dollars [7] by and among non-communist countries in Europe, the recovery of western Europe appeared to be a test case for the thesis that a healthy economy was synonymous with a healthy democracy.

To people who cared so much for economic recovery and stability, the dollar became the symbol of successful capitalist resistance to the disrupting forces of communism. It acquired a charismatic value which it has not yet completely lost, despite having undergone the indignity of devaluation. More important, European post-war reconstruction, the popular simplification of its problems of development in terms of dollar losses and acquisitions, helped to identify (with much stultification) the complexity of the Cold War defence-mechanism in Europe with the mechanism of the dollar gap, and later with the defence of the dollar.

Furthermore, it helped to strengthen the myth that the military and ideological assault on communism could be met with the help of a push-button, financial-military machine, a trend of thought against which J. R. Schlesinger warned when he wrote that 'the question we must face is whether or not the *contemporary* American emphasis upon economic capacity is not, in fact, over-emphasized, another example of the tendency, not restricted to the military, to fight the last war'.[8]

Reactions to American aid

It is only natural that an approach to development based on and motivated by economics should create conflicting attitudes towards the whole strategy of aid. Some Frenchmen, for instance, sincerely believed that the 'dollarization' of their economy could be kept separate from the 'dollarization' of their society. Others, like de Gaulle, fought hard to reduce the pre-eminence of the dollar, while *L'Express* editor, J.-J. Servan-Schreiber, showed in a best-seller how unfounded such a hope was.[9]

These hopes and resentments were by no means confined to Europeans, but accompanied American aid everywhere. An Indian, Mrs Ramma Pan, expressed them as early as 1952 when she wrote:

You [Americans] at the moment are concerned with a way of life. We are concerned with means of life. These, I am certain, you can produce for us. . . . As to the way of life, we have been concerned with this for 5,000 years . . . and it does not come to us as any shock. But it is fairly recently that it has occurred to America that this thing that they have built up during the last couple of centuries that they call 'The American Way of Life' is an expandable commodity, that it is something they ought to try to sell to the rest of the world.[10]

These were ominous words, to be repeated later, *ad nauseam*, in the new countries of the Third World.

However, the success achieved by the free world in the dollar gap battle, reinforced those who wanted to approach the problems of underdevelopment outside Europe in terms of financial aid. They worked out strategies aimed at achieving capital accumulation, price stability and balanced budgets, without sufficiently grasping the difference between the economic situation in post-war Europe and that of the underdeveloped countries. Poverty and underdevelopment were to be found in both cases, but whereas in the case of Europe it was a temporary, war-created poverty in an otherwise highly developed society, in the case of the new, extra-European countries it was the endemic poverty and stagnation of colonial territories. A new approach was therefore required.

Dr Gunnar Myrdal, speaking in Cairo in 1954,[11] called on the young economists of the Third World to provide the new leadership and the new imaginative strategies. He asked them to throw away 'the large structures of meaningless, irrelevant, and sometimes blatantly inaccurate doctrines and theoretical approaches and to start their thinking afresh from the study of their own needs and problems'. This, he said, would take them far beyond both the outdated western liberal economies and Marxism. Instead of 'chewing over' old doctrines and doctrinal controversies, many of them hundreds of years old or more, they should make their own theoretical construction to suit their problems. He was hardly heard. So little, in fact, that sixteen years later, in 1969, he could write an entire book – *The Challenge of World Poverty* (already mentioned) – to analyse the blunders which were made when routine, traditional, western economic systems were applied to non-western countries.

He was not the only unheard Cassandra in this field. Milton Friedman[12] shared his views, although he defended the more practical government approach to aid as against Myrdal's moral approach, since the role which he (Friedman) assigned to economic aid was to win over to one's own side those uncommitted nations which were also underdeveloped and poor. Nevertheless, Friedman rejected the logic of a free world – and more particularly a defender of free enterprise like the US – adopting what he considered the methods of the enemy, in the battle of development. If the aim and the interest of the US – he wrote – is that 'the underdeveloped countries chose the democratic rather than the totalitarian way of life, then the means of foreign aid should be adapted to the proposed aim – at least as far as economic aid proper is concerned'. Taking issue with the *Report submitted by the MIT Center for International Studies to the Special Senate Committee to study the Aid Program*, Friedman sets out the criteria suggested by this study for judging whether a country should be given additional aid by the USA. According to the report, the criterion should be the country's 'additional national effort' towards economic development. The two 'rules of thumb' for deciding whether this is the case, are – still according to the MIT report – 'the launching of measures to capture a good fraction of increase in income for the purpose of further investment', and second, the 'degree to which a country's leaders have worked out an overall development program'. So much for the report. By these standards, says Friedman, the USA would never have qualified as a country making an 'additional effort' towards economic development. In fact, he claims, the only countries that satisfy the tests suggested by the MIT report are the communist countries. These all have measures 'to capture a good fraction of increase in income for the purpose of further investment' and all have an 'overall development program'. Although, says Friedman, free enterprise has proved a far better system for promoting economic development than the Marxist, and has shown itself 'the only effective route to a rising standard of life for the masses of the people, and the only route consistent with political freedom and democracy', the MIT report, and most other writings on the subject, simply take the opposite for granted. This, says Friedman, is 'modern mythology with a vengeance'.[13]

Communist aid programmes

De-Stalinization and the communist policy of aiding development in non-communist countries, go hand in hand. Both presuppose the idea that 'competitive coexistence' is replacing the inter-bloc struggle for world supremacy. Such a policy could not have existed before 1953. In fact, it is only in 1954 that the Sino-Soviet bloc made its first commitment (eleven million dollars) to and first payment (one million dollars) towards economic assistance in developing countries.[14]

Despite communist inexperience in overseas colonial policies and in the distribution of aid to underdeveloped countries outside the socialist bloc, the communists enjoyed considerable advantages over the western world from the outset. Being unfettered, at least at the time, by the problem of nationalities inherited from Tsarist colonialism in Central and Eastern Asia, they could point an accusing finger at the colonial West with an apparently clear conscience. They could make good use of the traditional struggle of Marxism against colonialism. They could also offer the newly independent countries a successful model of agrarian reform, which had turned Russia and China from backward States into industrial powers, through their own anti-imperialist struggle. As soon as western colonial rule permitted it, the communist representatives moved about in the Third World with an ideological self-assurance, a revolutionary and historically deterministic confidence, and with an abruptness of publicly uncriticizable functionarism, which sent cold shivers down the spines of western politicians, former colonial officials, and new technical experts in charge of western aid programmes to underdeveloped countries. There were, of course, some exceptions. Some American political scientists looked with mixed feelings at the entry of the Soviet Union into the foreign aid arena. The Soviet aid competition imparted a fresh sense of challenge and urgency to a United States policy that was rapidly being weakened by frustration, doubt and disillusion. Joseph Berliner, one of the first American political writers to give a comprehensive description of Soviet aid to the developing world, saw the growing competition between the western and the communist blocs as a positive contribution, though for quite different reasons. The West, he wrote,[15] was committed, for a variety of reasons, to the encouragement of economic development and rising living standards in poor countries, but could not provide sufficient help by itself. The Soviet contribution towards this goal, therefore, should be greeted with warmth.

Other 'Cold War specialists', too, were not afraid of communist competition in aid to the developing world. James R. Schlesinger[16] felt that 'if the underdeveloped nations have envisaged the Soviet Union, in George Kennan's phrase, as the "horn of plenty", what could be more advantageous for us than for them to see how empty the horn is.'

Judging solely from the statistics, Schlesinger was correct. From 1954 to 1963, the cumulative total aid from the Sino-Soviet bloc to developing countries amounted to 5,393 million dollars in commitments, of which only 1,860 million dollars were actually disbursed.[17] This was a small fraction of the aid extended by the western world to underdeveloped countries. In 1963, for example, the Sino-Soviet bloc disbursed 425 million dollars, yet this was still less than 5 per cent of the flow of official resources from western countries. If one were to make an attempt at an assessment of the 'real value' of the burden of development loans, by estimating the discounted present value of future repayments, the Soviet programme covers roughly 1 per cent of the total OECD programme.[18]

However, the impact of the communist programme was out of all proportion to its economic value. Many ideological and methodological factors contributed to its success.

Seen from a world geopolitical point of view,[19] the former colonial, underdeveloped parts of the world (with some notable exceptions, e.g. Australia) represented the only available area of possible political competition left to the five 'Big Powers' which still existed – at different levels of effective or potential strength – at the conclusion of the Second World War. The 'Big Five' – USA, USSR, western Europe, China, and Japan – had several things in common: vast areas submitted to their political control or (as in the case of Japan) economic influence; control of raw materials and skilled manpower; ability to produce expensive modern military equipment, and – except in the case of Japan – multinational and/or multiracial composition. Furthermore, they were all situated in the same zone – between the thirtieth and sixtieth lines of latitude in the northern hemisphere. Whatever the advantages – climatic, historical, social or other – which this geographical deployment gave them, it was clear that the absence of empty spaces in this part of the world, combined with their possession of great industrial power, would make any attempt at horizontal expansion equivalent to military suicide. The forced coexistence imposed on these northern hemisphere powers by the 'balance of fear', a fear of total destruction, meant that unbridled 'competitive coexistence' was possible only in the areas below the thirtieth line of latitude, namely in that part of the world which included most of the underdeveloped, former colonial countries.

In these new arenas of the battle for international supremacy it was not only the means – economic or technical – which counted. It was the ability to export political utopias and ideological myths to support the equation – drawn by all competitors – between material development and a certain political ideology.

In this field, communism enjoyed great psychological advantages over the West. Quite apart from the world-wide applicability of its ideological tenets, it had succeeded – for the first time since the Turkish siege of Vienna in the eighteenth century – in putting western civilization on the defensive. Communism's mixture of political, military and ideological power, fascinated many western intellectuals and made them dream of a Soviet paradise, just as western intellectuals in the Middle Ages dreamt of the hospitable and tolerant pastures of Islam. This dream was encouraged by the prevention (in the fifties) of any expression of intellectual revolt within the communist bloc which would have demonstrated the existence of other 'clerics' believing that the 'tolerant green pastures' of modern society were to be found beyond the frontiers of communism.

For the majority of western people who rejected communism, the Marxist influence, extending 'like a menacing, radioactive cloud from Saxony to Shanghai',[20] produced a feeling of undefined rather than clear-cut dangers, thus giving the western world a feeling of insecurity which increased its own bad conscience towards the colonial peoples and thus the image of weakness and uncertainty which it projected beyond its own frontiers.

In the course of time, the communist challenge produced its own antidotes, which contributed to the revitalization of the democratic world. It gradually became more and more apparent that communist strength was weakened by the 'prostitution' of its own ideals of freedom and equality, and by the fundamental contradiction between the noble aims of individual and collective freedom and low and oppressive methods.

These antidotes, however, meant little to the rank and file of the Third World, where freedom from hunger and not freedom of ideas was the major preoccupation. Furthermore, the type of nationalism which animated the new nations of the world was totally different from the nationalism of the western world or of colonial America. It was a nationalism composed basically of economic and racial resentment against the West – a resentment which equated anti-colonialism with the 'western question'. The latter, in turn, was not dissimilar to the 'western question' which dominated Russian politics in the early part of the twentieth century.

It was in this sense that Adlai Stevenson expressed the feeling that it would be a catastrophe for the free world if the Americans were unable to take up the challenge of the developing world, if they could not identify themselves with 'this social and human revolution, to encourage aid, to inspire the aspirations of half of humanity for a better life, to guide these aspirations on the road of liberty'.[21]

Faced with such a 'crusading' view of the 'competitive coexistence' between western and communist worlds, it is hardly surprising that the majority of experts, particularly within the American administration, took a rather more eschatological view of the new confrontation, which they expressed in a whole series of Cassandra-like publications. Schlesinger,[22] for example, noted that the campaign to expose the economic threat represented by communist aid to the underdeveloped world was launched by the State Department early in 1958 – after the year of Bandung, we may note in passing. It is sufficient to glance at the titles of some official publications of the time to get the idea. Department of State Publication No. 6632 (Washington, D.C., 1958) was, for instance, entitled *The Sino-Soviet Economic Offensive in the Less-Developed Countries*; DSP No. 6777 (Washington, D.C., 1959) was entitled *The Communist Economic Threat*. Other, less official publications, such as Robert L. Allen's *Soviet Economic Warfare* (Washington D.C., 1960), took the same 'fighting' view of the problem, hoping to reverse earlier and more placid official attitudes which claimed, *inter alia*, that the Soviet bloc's economic activities were on too small a scale to be a source of concern. So much for communist ideology. Communist techniques also seemed to be superior to western ones.

Aid within the framework of the Cold War

The evaluation – evidently irrational – of the communist capacity to wage an aid-war in underdeveloped countries was probably one of the outcomes of the USA's political battle with communism, which had suffered a major defeat in one non-western underdeveloped country – China. This defeat stood against the USA's anti-communist victory in Europe, and increased the feeling that outside Europe the communists could be more efficient and more articulate than the 'defenders of the free world'. Their use of aid as a political tool – it was claimed – fitted better into the general pattern of their diplomatic and ideological strategy. The communists could impress the countries of the Third World with the example of the efforts made to transform their agrarian, quasi-colonial economies into industrial ones. They could also act in a simple, direct and cheap political way because – unlike the Americans – they did not have the responsibility of maintaining the *status quo*. On the contrary, they aimed everywhere at creating a 'revolutionary climate' in which the anti-western feelings of the colonial élites could best be exploited. They were free to participate in the national liberation movements and to help subversive groups, while maintaining their contact with the governments which these same movements or groups were trying to overthrow. Their aim was change for its own sake, and not concern with the maintenance of any established political situation. Finally, the communists, belonging to totally planned and government-controlled countries, were freer than the West to play with indigenous economies through the political motivated purchase of local surplus commodities.

The West – and the United States in particular – were usually burdened with the problem of maintaining an often unpopular *status quo*. Their military commitments were part of such policies, which could hardly be pursued without political strings. Their parliaments, especially the American House of Representatives, were jealous of their budget control over the administration, and did not permit the diplomats and experts in the field to commit the government to extended projects of help. They forced them to rely on shrinking, year-by-year allotments of funds. The fact that the free economic system of the West did not facilitate the bulk purchase of surpluses from underdeveloped countries seemed no less important. Decision- and policy-making processes in the West were slower than in communist countries, and often disrupted by the contradictions arising from internal political changes and multi-faceted, world-wide political involvement. Finally, the very connection between the idea of democracy and free enterprise sounded ominous to many peoples in former colonial areas – a new version of that unchecked exploitation which accompanied all colonial enterprises.

It was, therefore, with an inferiority complex made up of self-criticism, with a blend of fear and admiration for the monolithic power of the communist régimes, and with bureaucratic resentment on the part of aid administrators for the lack of understanding shown by their home governments for their own well-intentioned efforts, that many western plans for aid were put forward and many theories advanced as to the best way to adapt Western assistance to the underdeveloped countries. Most of these plans and theories suffered from being more of an answer to the challenge of communist penetration into the newly independent, underdeveloped countries, than to the real needs of the recipients. This approach made it difficult for many western donor countries to distinguish between the real *élan* of the aid offensive of the communists and the sharp-shooting propaganda techniques available to the Soviet bloc.

Edward S. Mason, writing in 1958, said that 'the myth of the American development ideology is the community development program, while the Soviet myth is the steel mill. There is little doubt which is more highly esteemed in most underdeveloped countries.'[23] It took a long time for this fetishist approach to communist aid to be reduced to more rational proportions. This was acknowledged in 1970 by John Kenneth Galbraith, who wrote:

It is fair to observe that Western concern for non-Communist development was matched by a Soviet anxiety for the opposite. Now, alas, we know that it does not matter. We know that the development will be so slow that the question of what ultimately emerges *is academic*. And in the interim, a jungle, whether a capitalist jungle or a Communist jungle, is still a jungle and the difference cannot be told by anyone walking through. And a desert, whether a capitalist or a Communist desert, is still most naturally a desert. And a poor peasant society, whatever it calls itself, is subject to the same cruel parameters of over-population, insufficient land, insufficient capital, insufficient education and technology that is limited by all these. And, to repeat, one cannot but imagine that the Soviets agree. Circumstances, if sufficiently obdurate and compelling, leave little open for ideological preference.[24]

However, despite much evidence, the inadequacies of the communist aid system are still much less apparent than the inadequacies of the West. This may be due, as Milton Friedman suggested, to the tendency of the West to cultivate 'modern mythologies with a vengeance'. Take, for instance, the myth that communist policy is simple, linear and free from inner contradictions. Many western observers have claimed that this was the strength of the communist system. It is true that the communist governments could make decisions more easily than the democracies. Nevertheless, communist aid was not linear nor free from contradictions – at least, not for the communists themselves. In 1952 Malenkov said that 'we are living in an age in which all roads lead to communism'; Chou En-lai promised that 'Africa is the continent ripe for revolution'. Both proved to be wrong. Communist miscalculations were due as much to contradictions in their theoretical and practical approach to problems of development as the fact that the 'Ugly American' had his 'Ugly Russian' counterpart.

At the time, there were strong ideological doubts at the Marxist end of the line (not yet a donor end) about the best way for communist countries to deal with the non-communist régimes of the underdeveloped world. Prior to the Bandung Conference in 1955, the nationalist leaders in the underdeveloped countries, particularly those in Africa, were frequently regarded by Moscow as 'bourgeois nationalists', not to be overly trusted. The Bandung Conference made it possible – and even necessary – for Russia to cooperate with 'the most varied parties and organizations' in the common struggle against colonialism.[25] This sometimes led to awkward situations, such as the butchering of the Communist Party in pro-Russian Sudan in 1971. The Conference certainly contributed to the Soviet departure from its previous policy of self-effacement *vis-à-vis* the Afro-Asian world. However, it would be quite wrong to think that such a change of policy was simply a tactical decision on the part of the Russians within the framework of their anti-western strategy. Whatever the immediate or long-term political aims, the elaborate theoretical discussion which the problem of collaboration with 'national bourgeoisies' in the developing countries elicited in the communist world was a very serious and soul-searching one. David Morison noted[26] that such a discussion was intended initially to justify the new Soviet attitudes and policies to the Soviet public itself. The ideological discussion of the questions why, how, and where to deal with the Third World is far from ended. The communists still feel quite uneasy about it today, despite the diplomatic and strategic justifications they may produce in the framework of their permanent struggle against 'capitalist imperialist aggression'.

To this day the communists have been unable to develop a consistent theory to guide them in their dealings with those countries which still live under the 'system of asiatic production'. This is the formula with which both Marx and Lenin described (without developing their views) those forms of production which 'precede capitalist production', and which are so prominent in the economies and social structures of the newly independent states of Africa and Asia.

It would be beyond the scope of this study to deal with the question of this concept – 'the system of asiatic production' – or with the history of theoretical and political arguments which the communists developed around it. It will suffice to recall that the violent debates and arguments which took place at the end of the twenties about the meaning of Marx's and Lenin's ideas on the 'system of asiatic production' led to the condemnation of the whole concept in 1931. This dogmatic decision was challenged, *inter alia*, by Karl Wittfogel,[27] who thus aroused waves of hatred against himself in the communist camp. Yet hate solves no problems, and the same dogmatism has been challenged more recently by a number of Marxist theoreticians who resent the subjection of historical materialism to a dogmatic philosophy of history.[28] The problem is not a purely speculative one: it is a very practical one, since the belief in the ability (or inability) to change pre-capitalistic societies into post-capitalist societies by going through, or not going through, the capitalistic stages of development, must have a direct influence on the whole conception of communist aid to underdeveloped countries. The practical consequence of Marxist questioning about the best way – other than through direct political control – to bring socialism to the Third World (a problem reminiscent of the soul-searching of the West about the best methods, other than colonial control, to 'make the underdeveloped countries progress'), seems to be this: the overwhelming majority of the responsible peoples in Asia, Africa and Latin America have begun to develop second thoughts about the applicability of both imported western and Marxist concepts of development to their own problems and requirements. There seems to be no real basis for those who believe that, provided economic growth continues at a certain given rate, western, Soviet bloc, and underdeveloped countries may eventually come to resemble each other.[29] Possibly in outward appearance, or in the use of the same technological gadgets, they may, but not in more fundamental aspects of their societies.

Inadequacies of both western and communist aid programmes
The situation in both East and West looks fairly equally balanced. In both camps theories of aid have proved inadequate. The idea that recipient will imitate donor has been refuted. Private initiative in economic development and industrialization does not necessarily create the conditions for democracy in the underdeveloped countries – chiefly because of lack of social spacing and stagnation, which transform all power relations into what Karl de Schweinitz calls the 'zero-sum-game'.[30] Equally, State capitalism does not necessarily favour communism. This is a fact which has been increasingly imposed on both western and communist authors. In no other part of the world where the battle of aid has been waged by the two blocs has it been so evident as in Africa. Here, independently of historical conditions and ideological sympathies, the major obstacle to proper utilization of aid-to-development has seemed to be the ignorance of (or at least the insufficient attention paid to) the effects of modernization on traditional societies.

In other words, the difference in the western and communist approaches to the problem of development of African societies is much more evident in the primary stages of the aid battle than in the subsequent ones. Once engaged, both blocs are troubled equally by the same dilemmas, doubts and inadequate tools for controlling the political effects of the aid extended. Perhaps the fact that dilemmas of aid are becoming more and more evident to communist experts makes them inclined to pay more attention to the practical and theoretical studies of their 'imperialist' colleagues. This attitude, of course, does not prevent the communists from preaching the advantages of Marxist dogmas and feeling free of the guilt complexes, the anguished doubts and the admitted inabilities of their western, democratic colleagues.[31]

Speaking in his capacity as US Ambassador, to an Indian audience, John Kenneth Galbraith gave a description of the contradictions involved in the process of economic development.

It is not that capital or technical training are unimportant or that planning is a waste of time. . . . The lesson is that we can no longer have one diagnosis of the causes of underdevelopment. . . . It goes without saying that we can no longer speak of a common prescription for development. Any effort to offer such a general formula will be productive only of waste, frustration and disappointment.[32]

If one compares such a statement with some of the economic certainties proclaimed by development economists before the year of Bandung, one can easily grasp the long path of doubts covered within a relatively short time by the people interested and involved in problems of underdevelopment.

A better realization and definition of the 'conditions and causes of underdevelopment' have made experts much more cautious about the chances of development of non-western societies on the basis of western experience. These experts have increasingly realized that economic development could be only one factor – sometimes even a secondary factor – in overall development. They began to understand that development for development's sake was not a universally accepted axiom. Development, in fact, was not a non-economic, value-free process, and the transfer of know-how could not be achieved independently of the transfer of wider intellectual concepts from donor to recipient countries. Since it was man who stood at the centre of the development process, the process itself must inevitably be a very complex, 'integrated' affair, raising a myriad considerations quite beyond the normal frame of interest and competence of one particular science. Considerations of this type encouraged many economists to turn themselves into sociologists, anthropologists or political scientists (often with dubious results), while anthropology, sociology and political science were, out of necessity, brought into the debates on economic development. None of this, however, led to the rapid emergence of an integrated system of research into the problems of development.

Trends in economic assistance since 1955

Whether real new insights have been gained by now is a debatable point, but no one can deny that conspicuous changes have taken place both in the theory and the practice of assistance to the development of underdeveloped areas, in the last sixteen years, namely since 1955.

The choice of that particular year as the starting point of the present study may appear arbitrary, since it was not marked by the appearance of any imposing work on development, or on the developing countries, such as the publication of Lord Hailey's *Survey of Africa* in 1938. Nor was it marked by the traumatic experiences of the First or Second World Wars, which destroyed the myth of the aristocratic unity of the white man in the Black Continent and disclosed his weakness and the new potentialities of Africa. However, 1955 was relevant in another respect: it was the year of the Bandung Conference, that emotional gathering of the 'have-nots' which gave younger nations in the furthest corners of the world the feeling that a new era was born.

For the leaders of the Third World, such as Nasser, Nehru, Sukarno and Chou En-lai, Bandung was a moment of historical triumph. For victorious communist China, Bandung was the consecration of her new leading role in Asia, no longer chaperoned by 'white' Soviet Russia, whose exclusion from the Afro-Asian meeting prodded her into involving herself more deeply in the battlefield of international cooperation. No less important for the evolution of future techniques of international aid was the exclusion of another country – Israel – from the Bandung meeting. The shock waves of Bandung did, in fact, hit Tel-Aviv more quickly and more deeply than Washington or London, and with results which we shall discuss in a later chapter.

Since the year of Bandung, 1955, theories and practices of international aid to underdeveloped countries have been changing radically, even in countries like the USA, where methods of assistance were so strongly influenced by the experience of American aid to Europe. The appearance of independent African countries on the scene of international relations, the eruption of the Cold War into the field of development aid, the growing realization – in both the West and the communist camp, of the inadequacy of economic theories to cope with the problems of underdevelopment, especially in Africa, forced even the most reluctant experts to rethink the strategy of aid in terms of the new situational logic.

Some mistakes in Economic Aid

The belief that foreign aid promotes economic development, writes Friedman, rests on three basic propositions: first, that the key to economic development is the availability of capital; second, that underdeveloped countries are too poor to provide the capital for themselves; and third – a point mentioned earlier – that centralized and comprehensive economic planning and control by government is an essential requisite for economic development.

In Friedman's view, all three propositions are misleading half-truths: additional capital is certainly essential for development, but the way in which capital is employed will also affect other things. The Pharaohs, for example, raised enormous capital to build the pyramids, which certainly did not promote economic development in terms of self-sustaining growth of the standard of life of the Egyptian masses. Modern Egyptian capital, under government auspices, built a steel mill, and this involved capital formation; nevertheless, the result was unsatisfactory. The mill was a drain on the economic resources of Egypt and not a contribution to economic strength: the cost of producing steel in Egypt is very much higher than the cost of buying it elsewhere. Hence, says Friedman, the mill is a mere modern equivalent of the pyramids, except that the maintenance cost is higher.[33]

So much for the first half-truth. With regard to the second, that underdeveloped countries are too poor to save and provide capital for themselves, Friedman asks the question, whence came the capital of the developed countries, which, once upon a time, before being developed, were obviously underdeveloped? His answer to this is that 'the key problem is not one of probability but of incentives and of proper use'. As an example of the improper use of capital he recalls that India, which for centuries was a storehouse of precious metals, did not develop because little of the savings took the form of productive accumulation. 'If other conditions for economic development are ripe,' he claims, 'capital will be readily available; if they are not, capital made available is very likely to be wasted.'

As for the third half-truth – 'economic development requires centralized government control and planning, that is, it requires a coordinated "development programme"' – government, in

Friedman's view, certainly has an important role to play in the process of development, but 'economic development is a process changing old ways of doing things and venturing into the unknown'. As such, it requires a maximum of flexibility, of possibility for experimentation. No one can predict in advance what will turn out to be the most effective use of a nation's productive resources. Yet the essence of a centralized programme of economic development is that it introduces rigidity and inflexibility. It involves a certain decision about what activities to undertake and the use of central force and authority to enforce conformity with that decision.

Even if Professor Friedman's reliance on private initiative was not the best remedy against underdevelopment, his criticism was, at least, cogent. However, it bore little fruit because, among other reasons, most people engaged in aid activities preferred to lend an ear to the claims of a growing legion of economic development experts who, deeply conscious of the importance of their promotion to the ranks of practical politicists (mainly because of the implications of the European economic recovery), trumpeted the world-wide validity of their theories for producing 'take-offs', 'big pushes', and 'de-establicized' and 'balanced growth' models of all kinds.[34]

This was the outcome of the logic of the situation; not only of the European post-war situation, but also of the growing interest of outstanding economists in the emerging world. To break the vicious circle of economic stagnation, to overcome the reality (inacceptable to colonial countries on the eve of political independence) of Nurkse's statement that 'a country is poor because it is poor',[35] to find the 'golden formula' of economic development for the underdeveloped, was a challenge which no economist could refuse to face, even if it led him into the unknown and dangerous ground beyond the field of western economics (itself not yet fully understood and controlled).

It quickly became apparent, however, that more than economic theory and economic experience was required to deal with problems of underdevelopment. If we find, therefore, on the eve of African independence, twelve years after the inauguration of the USA's Technical Assistance Program, that studies on development[36] invariably reveal that far from catching up, the underdeveloped countries were falling further and further behind, the cause is an intellectual shortcoming, the failure of an idea, and not a lack of goodwill. These analyses of the conditions of backwardness and of the ubiquity of vicious circles of underdevelopment were indeed accompanied by a 'renewed effort to devise policies and strategies for economic development'. But all this offered very little guidance to the harassed planner or programming officer in the underdeveloped countries. All they could state, in very general terms, was the rather obvious truth that 'capital formation is a good thing; that a little more of it is better than a little less – as is usually the case with a good thing – and that it matters little what special pattern of capital formation is selected, provided one does not go the whole hog in a single direction.' [37]

The inapplicability of some economic models
There was also a more important, though less evident, reason for the economist's difficulty in adapting himself to the realities of the new nations, which was pointed out by Professor Raoul Prebish in his introduction to the *Economic Development of Latin America and its Principal Problems*,[38] namely, the false idea that the economic model for the free market is universally applicable. In the case of the West, this mistake led to the protracted attempt to apply a purely monetary definition of the idea of profit to non-European countries. Similarly, in the case of the communist world, there was the equally protracted attempt to apply to non-European economies a purely European interpretation of history and economic class struggle which made little sense in colonial pre-industrial – and sometimes even pre-agricultural – societies.[39]

On the whole, both western and communist approaches to aid – at least in the first decades of operation – accepted with some variations a *credo* based on an analysis of past economic trends and projection of those required for the future. This search for an overall rational plan led to many aid battles, over and above the ideological and political battles between competing donor governments. What should be developed first, agriculture or industry? How should one deal with traditional societies? Should one use their élites as channels of gradual development, or bypass them by promoting new modernizing indigenous élites, educated in an alien, western culture? And where was the 'crucial swing role in modernizing politics' to be located: in the revolutionary cities or in the revolutionary villages? For a Leninist – but also for a bourgeois Frenchman – the answer to this last question would have been obvious. However, at two widely separated poles, and in totally different circumstances, the experience of China and of Israel could have shown that a strong push for innovation, change and modernization can come from the countryside just as much as from the city. Professor Huntington believes that while the role of the city is constant and a source of permanent opposition, the role of the countryside is variable and ambivalent: it can either be a source of stability or of revolution.

The (unsuccessful) search for an 'overall plan' of development had another, no less important, result. It led to a heightened consciousness, among the people involved in aid-to-development, of the simple fact that the less developed a country is, the more the planning depends on non-economic factors. What remained, perhaps, less clear to the vast mass of experts and advisers, was the fact that the more advanced economic planning is, the less capable it is of incorporating non-economic elements.

It thus became evident that any planning had to take into consideration many variables, the importance and meaning of which could be established only with the help of social sciences. The need to switch the focus of aid-to-development activities from 'environment' to 'man' – from – say – agriculture, to the agriculturist, became increasingly felt. One thing which development economists must recognize is that economic behaviour is conditioned by a cultural matrix which differs from society to society. Although much lip service has been paid to the social sciences in the formulation of technical assistance programmes, the potential of anthropology, for example, has not yet been fully exploited.

The impact of the social sciences

The days when an anthropologist like Sir James Fraser could say 'Heaven forbid!' to the idea of personally conducting field research among natives, or when E. E. Evans-Pritchard could say over the BBC (in 1950) that he did not attach much importance to any service that social anthropologists might bring to the solution of the problems of administration, have certainly gone. The day envisaged by Professor Radcliff-Brown, when with the more rapid advance of pure science itself and with the cooperation of colonial administrations, it would be possible to turn the government and education of the native peoples in various parts of the world into an art based on the application of discovered laws of anthropological science, has certainly not yet arrived. 'Discovered laws of anthropological science' have not yet been discovered, and in the field of social development we are still without a general theory of social mutation, despite the many new ideas advanced in the field. This last fact has not prevented the formulation of many methods of 'social engineering', particularly by western development experts in non-western societies.

A readiness to meet natives, however, was not enough. It was a proof of good intentions, but no substitute for a comprehensive new approach to aid which would make man himself, and not the economic or ideological control of his environment and behaviour, the focus of international efforts of cooperation. There was no idea in the offing: under the pressure of the Cold War and the political exigencies of the 'battle of aid', the manipulators of aid programmes and their mentors worked without any guide-lines. They switched from the economic approach of the pre-Bandung years to the socio-political approach of the post-Bandung era, finding themselves drifting towards the viewpoint against which Friedman had warned: the need for growing State intervention in development.

In any new country, of course, the State is the most important, the most reliable, and frequently the sole employer. It is therefore natural that much depends on the relationship which the individual establishes with the State, quite apart from his political convictions or professional abilities. However, this does not necessarily mean that development could benefit by direct government intervention. In fact it could be hindered more than helped, since it is almost impossible to detach government intervention from a growing application of authority in fields like innovation and invention (essentials for the absorption of aid and the diffusion of modernization) in which the use of authority is the obstacle to the process of development itself.

This point, too, will be discussed in detail in the following chapter. Here, I wish to stress that, because the relationship between authority and innovation was not clearly understood by the people dealing with government aid, it was inevitable that they should permit international cooperation to become almost exclusively a matter of inter-governmental relations. This trend magnified the political aspect of modernization, and produced many new theories and models of aid which – alas – soon proved to be ineffective.

The overwhelming importance attached to the political factor in development, when observed by students of the subject (who frequently wrote books in order to support the political efforts of their own – communist or capitalist – countries), gave rise to a tendency in the literature which tended to equate political progress – even when understood in diametrically opposed ways by Marxists and non-Marxists – with economic and social progress. Whatever this may have meant for people in the underdeveloped countries, the expression 'political development' was used so often by students of modernization in the sixties that it became a euphemism, devoid of any analytical meaning and therefore a cause of much confusion.

Partly as a consequence of the theory which closely linked economic progress with political integration, and political integration with nationalism, a tendency developed among students of development which led to a reversal of the original line of thought. It was believed by some experts in modernization that by creating national integration – even in cases such as Nigeria or Palestine, where there was little 'integrative' connection between the various social, geographical or political frames to which people were attached – one could promote political modernization and, through this, economic and social change. The integrative, functionalist analysis of the process of development, understood as a political process, found expression in the works of G. A. Almond. In his introduction to *The Politics of Developing Areas* (1960) Almond defines the political system as carrying out, in every society, 'the functions of integration and adaptation', through the threat of the actual use of legitimate constraint. This was stretching the concepts of both development and politics, and elicited several reactions.[40]

Professor S. Huntington was one of the American political writers to expose the fallacy of the equation between political and non-political modernization.[41] He pointed out that mobilization and participation, produced by increased literary organism or industrialization in non-developed countries, do not necessarily follow the patterns of mobilization and participation processes in industrialized countries. Yet even Huntington clearly puts stability forward as a major objective and factor of modernization, to the extent that he seems to value communist stability more than frail democracy in developing countries.[42]

Believers in 'political development' also very often overlooked the time element, that is, the length of time during which political changes took place in the industrialized countries of the world, and are now taking place in the underdeveloped ones. In Lucy Mair's words:

The changes which African societies are going through are not in essence different from those which the European societies have experienced as the mass of their population ceased to be peasants or craftsmen and became agricultural labourers and machine-minders. What makes changes in Africa so striking is their speed. As one reads the history of the 18th century, the 17th, the 16th and even further back, one can find parallels with contemporary events on that continent. . . . But the most striking contrast between the experience of Africa and the history of Europe lies in the fact that from medieval times the rulers of Europe have been able to command the service of literate persons to meet the need of administration as conceived at any given time; there has been a graduation rather than a gulf in the outlook and mode of life between literate and illiterate. In Africa the gulf is real and deep. The top people are those who have been educated in schools giving the instruction in the language of the metropolitan power. Not all of them have had a secondary education; only a few have had more. From them come the politicians, the professionals, the civil servants, the technicians. . . . The difficulty of adequately staffing the public services and industry without recourse to the 'expatriates' is everywhere considerable. The new élites are the people whose mode of life is thoroughly Westernized as far as the externals are concerned, who live in brick and cement houses and own cars and refrigerators and they are the sources of nationalist leadership and political ideas.[43]

The same could be said for other underdeveloped societies in all parts of the world.

European ethnocentricity

There is a growing feeling that many of the solutions proposed or tried have not worked because they had – as in medieval exorcism – little relation to the disease which they were intended to cure, and this for two main reasons: the first, understandable and quite legitimate, is that a problem at once so complex and so novel requires more time, more research and more failures, before it can advance the science (or sciences) of aid-to-development. The second reason, also understandable but less legitimate, is a persistent attitude of superiority in many people dealing with development problems and aid, in both developed and underdeveloped countries.

We know so little about man in general, and about the man who belongs to societies which have developed outside the historical and philosophical framework of the western world in particular, that we tend to analyse his problems more and more from the outside, to describe them rather than to try and identify with them. This 'outside' attitude is expressed in terms of subjective western experience, according to a rationale which is usually very different from that of the people of non-western cultures. We try to overcome this difficulty by the use of formulas as general and as abstract as possible, but the more these formulas – whether economic, political or sociological – are applied, the more they create a situation similar to that of a person who 'having repeated twenty times the word "travel" in succession, has become fully aware of the motions of the tongue and of the sound involved in saying "travel", but dissolves the meaning of the word itself'.[44]

One still finds this attitude deeply engrained in the educational systems of the newly independent countries and widely used by expatriate administrators of aid-to-development. One of the most current phrases one finds in the mouths of technical advisers – especially when speaking among themselves – is: 'Instead of messing things up in their own way, why don't they just copy carefully what we try to teach them to do?' It would be wrong to attribute such a 'blimpish' approach to outdated colonialism, though this colonial and patronizing mentality still exists among many members of the aid agencies. It is part and parcel of a much wider phenomenon: that of the unique universal diffusion of European civilization, and its equation with modern progress.

The Europeans are certainly not the only 'race' of men who have spread far beyond their indigenous borders. The people of Polynesia and Melanesia spread out over immense areas, carrying their customs, their technology and – as in the case of Madagascar – their language with them for thousands of miles. But the white man has enveloped the whole world with the influence either of his physical presence or of the products of his all-powerful technology. The fact that in his view material development and progress appeared, if not identical, at least to have a very considerable degree of overlap and feedback between them, only strengthened his feeling of universalism and self-confidence in his own way of life. His experience as a member of an expanding civilization was totally different from that of members of other migratory societies. Unlike them, he 'has never seen an outsider, perhaps, unless the outsider has already been Europeanized. The uniformity of customs, of outlook that he sees spread about him, seem convincing enough and conceal from him the fact that it is often all an historical accident'.[45] It is difficult for western expatriates, even the best-intentioned, to extricate themselves from this egocentric psychological situation. Often they cannot count on the help of their own social theorists to distinguish clearly between their own customs and those of the people whom they are supposed to be helping to develop within their own setting, because until recently custom 'did not challenge the attention of social theorists, because it was the very stuff of their own thinking: it was the lens without which they could not see at all'.[46]

It should not be forgotten, however, that the instinctive feeling of superiority of the western expert in aid-to-development is paralleled by an equally instinctive feeling of dependence in the recipient of the aid. The latter feeling may often be accompanied by a sense of inferiority, but one should distinguish carefully between the two, at least for the purpose of improving techniques of aid. Any person who has known Africa before and after independence will, I think, appreciate the contribution of political freedom to the dignity of the formerly colonized native, and the speed with which inferiority complexes are wiped out – sometimes more than wiped out – by the process of Africanization in all aspects of national life, and in spite of the numerous cries of 'neo-colonialism'.

The same cannot, however, be said about the feeling of dependence. To use Abram Kardiner's definition (which he, of course, applied in the context of child behaviour), dependence is that situation with which a person feels he cannot cope, accompanied by a recognition (conscious or unconscious) of the limitations of his resources and an expectation of outside aid. With the child, claims Kardiner,

> one of the most important influences which tend to perpetuate this attitude of timidity and dependence is failure in the newer types of adaptation: dependence really signals the continuation of the inhibitory effects of failure. . . It has been found that in the development of new techniques, which are in a constant state of change, failures are frequent. At this juncture, magic help is likely to be revived.[47]

Conflict between conceptual categories

Nothing is further from my mind than the belief that non-western peoples are like children, and that it is possible to understand them best by applying to them the concepts of child psychology, in particular that school which is based on observation of the western child. But insofar as industrialization and technical progress are often regarded – even if wrongly – as development itself, and not as an aspect of development; and insofar as techniques of technical progress are taught to non-western adults by people who were trained to teach them to western children or youth, or who regard the recipients of this more advanced know-how as 'children' *vis-à-vis* the techniques themselves, it is clear why people in underdeveloped countries accept aid more passively than actively. They do not 'digest' it; they do not remould it according to their own logic and understanding. The aid is given according to the logic of the donors, not because the donors lack the goodwill or the imagination to see the recipients' point of view – imagination is still in demand with the aid-to-development agencies – but because the new techniques, the fast-changing know-how, the innovations to be transferred, have their origin almost without exception in the western tradition of thinking, and therefore impose their own logic on the process of transfer, unhampered by any attempt to

adapt them to another type of thinking. Whether they are transferred as 'black boxes', or are accepted as understood techniques
(which, because they are understood, impress the people who
receive them with the speed of their constant changes) development processes and organized aid for its promotion seem to provoke some of the reactions which have been noticed in children
exposed to quick changes: dependence and a reliance on 'magic'.

All these are well-known facts; well-known, at least, to the
anthropologist and the psychologist, well before the idea of organized aid-to-development became an integral part of modern international relations. The fact that for many years the people
responsible for aid to underdeveloped societies have neglected the
advice of the 'students of men', preferring to rely on that of the
'students of environment', and particularly the economists, has
already been referred to, together with the obvious problems which
it aroused both in the 'free world' and in the communist camp.
These habits and attitudes are changing only very slowly – if at
all. They have been institutionalized in international or national
organizations, in which – as the Jackson Report, mentioned above,
noted in connection with UN agencies – the 'machine' of the
organization tends to become uncontrollable, and to acquire all
the agility and flexibility of a prehistoric monster.

Assuming, however, for the sake of argument, that a new,
broader approach to aid-to-development is beginning to crystal-
lize, the big question remains: at what point in the process of
promoted development is it most economical or effective to apply
this new approach? My belief is that the carrier of innovation is
the best point of impact, and I shall try, in the next chapter, to
explain why.

Chapter 3

Micro-Cooperation
versus
Macro-Cooperation

The concept of progress

A few exceptions notwithstanding,[1] there seems to be a general consensus, among donor and recipient countries, that development is both necessary and good. There is far less agreement about the aims of development and the methods necessary to bring it about. That aims and methods should be the source of acrid debate among developed and developing nations is natural, since there are at least as many targets of international cooperation as there are States and international organizations involved in it. Part of the debate – and much of the misunderstanding – also stems from the fact that the meaning of progress fostered by aid is unclear. Modern progress is commonly understood as economic advance through technological progress. Technology is neutral inasmuch as it consists, strictly speaking, of laboratories, machinery and processes which exist objectively and can therefore be transferred, bought, sold, like any other transferable commodity. It is neutral also because

... though historically associated with the type of economy generally known as Western capitalism, technology by its intrinsic nature transcends all social forms, the whole heritage of acquired institutions and habits. It serves with impartiality Japanese samurai, American industrialists and the Russian Soviet state. Universal in its reach, it cannot be monopolized by any nation, class, period, government or people. In catholicity it surpasses religion.[2]

That is one aspect of progress: at the same time, the idea of modern progress due to the spread of technology has another meaning which is far from neutral. The moment a traditional society opens itself to modern progress, the traditional values and the traditional leadership on which that society has rested, lived and received guidance, are pushed aside. The warrior, the priest and the political leader sink into the background or operate only in accordance with the economic realities produced by the machine.

Progress and authority

The dilemma which then faces developing countries is obvious: progress weakens the prestige, the 'imitative hold' of those leaders whose behaviour has for generations set the pace for the behaviour of the masses. Nowhere is this phenomenon more evident than in Africa. Here modernization does not mean an encounter between a higher level of development and a lower one (as is the case with north and south Italy). Nor does it represent the encounter between a higher level of western development with a lower, though culturally strong, level of non-western development (as in the case of Japan and India). In Africa the all-powerful process of modernization introduced mainly through colonial conquest, clashes on unequal terms with the patterns of indigenous cultures which are weak in every sense.

The traditional representatives of these weak cultures have seen their authority curtailed by a two-pronged attack. On the one hand there was the foreign administration, which suppressed their effective independence and reduced their prestige even when the presence of the European power beside the native chief extended his influence.[3] On the other hand there were the new and rising indigenous élites, promoted through western educational, military, economic and religious systems, who also challenged their traditional authority. Post-independence Africa has thus witnessed the generalized phenomenon of indigenous traditional chiefs fighting or being fought by the new indigenous government more fiercely than the colonial authority. This is an understandable phenomenon. Colonial officials, despite battles with a few chiefs, did not consider them as rivals, since the metropolitan sources from which they drew their authority were totally different from the sources of authority of the chiefs. They ruled, but did not compete. The new African leaders, who have replaced the colonial officials, find themselves, however, in direct competition with the traditional chiefs, battling for the same sources of indigenous support.[4] These chiefs are today often offered, by the newly independent African régimes, the alternative – but not always the choice – of being absorbed into the new African and imported system of political, administrative, educational, religious or ideological rule (as in the case of Ivory Coast or Uganda). In some cases the alternative is simply to disappear. In neither case is the alternative an easy one for either new indigenous rulers or traditional chiefs. The switch from one type of authority to another is always a long process, activated not by governmental will but by a complicated social logic of its own, which generally defies all attempts at political planning. It is, in fact, relatively easy to replace a foreign governor and his officials with an indigenous head of State and his ministers and functionaries. The number of people involved in a switchover of this kind is relatively small and the appeal of power remunerative and attractive. It is much more difficult either to alter the attitudes of family heads or clan leaders, whose traditional influence on the people is strong because of their physical proximity to the source of their authority. An authority, moreover, which is the more effective since it is justified by rooted religious beliefs and social conventions, and not just by economic, administrative, or ideological considerations. I shall return to this point later in the book. The point I wish to make here is that the traditional African chief offers a good example of some of the major differences distinguishing modern from traditional authority.

Modern authority, even in the most authoritarian régimes, needs to be shared, if only because of its own practical requirements. Traditional authority – even when it is delegated by the chief to 'the speaker of the tribe' or – as often happened in earlier times – to a slave, is never divided. In many parts of Africa the main characteristic of the traditional chief's authority has been that he acted 'generation after generation [as] leader of the army, judge, political sovereign and master of home affairs. . . At the core of his authority is a spiritual quality which a stranger cannot apprehend and may not touch. . . The very life of the country is dependent on the chief.'[5] If one succeeds in building an administration around the real chief, 'the whole population will be included', says French colonial governor Robert Delavignette, and this because, independently of whether the chief is old, blind or illiterate, the only thing which counts and which does not depend on education, age or health, is the 'sacred character of power'.[6]

For an anthropologist like Max Gluckman,[7] this unity can also be a direct function of the level of technology used in a given society. The 'dominant characteristic of a tribal society,' he writes, is that such a society has 'primary goods only and no luxuries.' A man with a thousand head of cattle could not use all the milk, meat and skins himself. The fact that he uses them to attract and support dependants and thus acquire power is a process not fundamentally different from the investment of wealth in a modern society in order to gain the right to demand goods and services from other people. What is different, stresses Gluckman, is the fact that in a modern society, investment is done through a system of *impersonal* relations, while in a traditional society, investment is done almost exclusively through a system of *personal* relations. Furthermore, a low level of technology 'makes it easier to move people to food than food to people', while the ability of men to produce – because of their low technological level – only a 'little beyond what they can consume, makes impossible the employment of the poor by the rich in order to give the rich an elaborate level of life above that of the poor'.

'An Emir of the Moors' – wrote Delavignette (though he could equally well have been referring to an Emir in Kuweit or a cabinet minister in Africa) – 'who lives in a house in St Louis-in-Senegal, who gets into his car and visits his tribe, is no longer a chief in the native sense of the word. He may well be a progressive man but in fact he leaves the people without a chief. It is not from a house that he can govern tents: it is not in a car that he can be understood by a community of camel drivers. The secret of [this] simplicity, unity, solidarity is still to be found in the village',[8] where the primary source of traditional authority still lies. However, when traditional leaders are unwilling, or incapable, of turning themselves into active participants in the process of modern development, they become either obstacles to progress, or irrelevant to it, or both at once.

In any of these three cases of 'non-progressive' leaders, the masses find themselves in trouble. They are faced with a choice between a foreign leadership which delivers the material goods of progress often without possessing the legitimacy to do so, and incompetent native leadership, which may still retain the legitimacy of authority but can no longer claim the right to lead.

In the dispute concerning the contrast between 'progressive' and 'reactionary' leadership in underdeveloped societies, there is a tendency to equate political 'progress' which is a matter of subjective opinion, with material progress. The dispute is a spurious one, since an alleged 'reactionary' can be turned into a so-called 'progressive' by being given the chance to act by his own lights, by removing the frustration that foreign aid causes him. Ideological, progressive, political radicalism, on the other hand, is no substitute for technological, progressive leadership. It may quite often even be an obstacle to progress, inasmuch as 'progressive régimes' which lack the political legitimacy of the traditional rulers, have to support their authority with authoritarian systems (*inter alia*, the strict control of information and of intellectuals) which hamper the diffusion of technological knowledge. However, (a) the artificial maintenance in power of technologically inefficient traditional authority, or (b) the substitution of technologically efficient but imported foreign authority, fares no better than a technologically incompetent native leadership, however progressive or conservative it happens to be. The first case usually leads to a situation of technological protectorate, the second to a situation of technological colonialism. Both lead to that widespread feeling of resentment, dissatisfaction and frustration, which is also common among many staff members of modern international cooperation. These feelings find expression in mutual accusations of ingratitude and of neo-colonialism.

If the idea of progress is at one and the same time both an interpretation of history and a philosophy of action, it is obvious that developing countries who support this idea cannot escape its philosophical implication, namely that Providence can be replaced by Change. But there is no reason why they should learn, together with western technology, to interpret history in a western manner. An indigenous interpretation of modern history requires indigenous interpreters. In order to make sense and to possess an appeal to the masses, the proper legitimacy of this interpretation of history must be seen and recognized – for better or for worse. Thus, even if the indigenous traditional leadership is technically and technologically inefficient, its role in underdeveloped countries is still important. The case of the African chief described above would seem to illustrate its value, at least for the purpose of finding the justifying interpretation of new historical processes of progress in terms of existing tradition. If this thesis is correct, there is no need for the innovator or the carrier of aid either to bow to indigenous leadership or to push it aside. It will be enough to recognize its dynamism and search for the best ways to channel it towards the desired goals, in its own situational logic and with some outside help. This is what I offer under the name of micro-cooperation.

Micro-cooperation

By micro-cooperation I mean that type of coordinated effort of international – bilateral or multilateral – help, which directs its efforts at encouraging man to change his patterns of productive activity in order to change his environment, rather than helping him to change his environment in order to change his way of life and production.

Further, micro-cooperation is an effort of cooperation among States, not just an effort of self-help within a given society, based on the fact that in the field of development techniques, some societies have accumulated more experience than others. However, whereas standards of technical cooperation are usually linked with the standard of development reached in a given country (those which are more advanced usually being able to teach more), the ability to extend micro-cooperation is not necessarily so. Smaller or less developed countries, which have developed rapidly in contemporary times, may have more to offer in the field of micro-cooperation than big powers.

Finally, micro-cooperation is a special pattern of *micro-aid*, for two reasons: first, because it requires less initial capital investment in terms of funds and goods; second – and this is the main point – because it is aimed essentially to influence the individuals within their own particular, established social setting, and not to influence their environment. For example, micro-cooperation does not deal with the development of agriculture – although this may be the final aim of a project – but with the development of the agriculturists who are participating in a given project. Obviously, micro-cooperation by itself cannot achieve much : as an integrated element of macro-cooperation, however, it becomes a powerful catalyst of latent energies. It helps to fire the minds and fantasies of the people who are, after all, the recipients of and the justification for any aid-to-development.

The basic concept underlying micro-cooperation is certainly not new. It was expressed many centuries ago by the Chinese philosopher, Kuan Tzu, who said: 'If you give a man a fish, he will have a single meal: if you teach him how to fish, he will eat all his life.'* The people involved in aid-to-development (i.e. macro-cooperation) are not unaware of this idea – quite the contrary. Almost all the studies and publications about cooperation stress the vital importance of considering the 'human side' of the problem. They say little about how this should be done in practice, nor do they seem receptive to advice in this field. The poor of the world, who could teach us something about how poor people should be treated, are not usually asked to do so (who has ever heard of Africans helping the Americans to solve their 'Negro problem'?) or do not have the means to do so. The rich, especially when they are also 'big powers', or think they have to act according to prestige images of themselves, operate through institutions the members of which seem to suffer from a common major disease – impatience. It is an understandable disease. Even when people are not driven by material philosophies – like those of the administrations who believe that it is possible to change the life of men just by changing their means of production – they prefer to deal with 'objects' rather than 'subjects'. It is infinitely less frustrating (though often more expensive) to operate with means than with men. Means can be replaced as many times as required, provided money is available (the way the Americans have run and lost the war in Vietnam is a superb example of such an approach). Men, especially if valuable, cannot.

This situation does not necessarily have to continue. In the world today, after twenty years of intensive effort in aid-to-development, there is a deep consciousness of the problem and a growing desire to search for a solution. What is lacking is the

---

* Adopted by J.-J. Servan-Schreiber, as an appropriate motto for his book, *The American Challenge*.

existence of a recognized and coherent approach to the problem of *the activation of men within their own social setting*, as an integral part of any project of aid-to-development.

This approach, I repeat, is what I call 'micro-cooperation', not so much in contradistinction to other types of cooperation, but as an indispensable part of any effort to transfer know-how. Indispensable in the sense that the distributor or the carburettor of a car is, to the engine. The very logic of the transfer of cultures calls for this approach.

Élite structures and the transfer of knowledge

There is a major difference between the process of acculturation inside a society and that of transculturation between two societies, especially when they are at different levels of development. In the case of acculturation, the process is a transfer of knowledge and authority from the élites of one generation to those of the next, without intermediaries. In the case of transculturation, the process is made less direct by the appearance of the 'man-in-the-middle', linking the donor and recipient societies.

The concept of the 'élite' has evolved from its original Latin meaning – 'chosen' – and in current political and sociological language means 'eminent'. Élite has been understood as being almost synonymous with class (Pareto); as a self-conscious unit with its particular entitlements, duties and rules of conduct (Nadel); as the holder of high positions in a given society (Easton Rothwell). Whatever the definition, it is the 'deference' of the non-élite towards the élite which distinguishes the latter from the former. The term 'deference', writes Thom Kerstiens, in his study, *The New Élite in Asia and Africa*,[9] is generally used to describe a situation whereby respect is paid to someone or some group because of generally recognized superior qualities, the possession of which is sought after as a benefit. But it is essential that deference should not be paid to an élite for one particular quality, such as superior knowledge or wealth, but that the superiority of the élite be more widely generalized. In an ideal situation, an élite would be respected for its general pattern of living. This last point is, quite rightly, considered essential by Kerstiens, since 'to exercise an influence, the qualities of an élite must be, to a certain extent, imitable'.[10]

In order to diffuse innovations, the ability to promote imitation is the essential quality in a traditional élite which must be activated through the techniques of micro-cooperation discussed in this book. This particular quality is recognized by all authors dealing with élites. The distinction made by Pareto – and others – between 'a governing élite, comprising individuals who directly or indirectly play some considerable part in the government, and the non-government élite, comprising the rest'[11] is, of course, valid for any society, developed or traditional. What seems to confuse the issue in the case of developing countries is the widespread belief that 'the identification of the political leadership group with the élite is particularly pertinent in the case of the developing countries which have recently acceded to independence'.[12] This identification, correct though it may be, does not create, in my view, an adequate feeling of 'deference', capable of promoting imitation in non-political fields of innovation. This is an important factor in the process of transmission of knowledge within a society and between societies at different levels of development.

In an integrated society, in a developed, western country, the élite will normally consist of the politicians, executives, army 'brass', religious and intellectual leaders, and so on. In a traditional, non-western society – for instance, in an African tribe – they will be the chiefs, the elders, the witch doctors and the artisans, who carry the secrets of their trades.

If (without attaching any value-judgement to the sign) we indicate the élite of the older generation in an integrated developed society by a plus sign (+) and the élite of the younger generation with another plus sign, we could say that the transfer of culture, in its widest form, follows a direct pattern in a process of selection and co-option. This pattern is more evident and more respected in a traditional, integrated society, in which the age factor is of importance. Through initiation practices (another form of examination), members of one generation pass on their selected and accumulated experience to the younger generation. The elders elect those whom they think are best for a job; they co-opt into their ranks the best – or those so considered – of the next generation, and once more we have a combined process of selection and co-option which can be schematically reproduced with a linear movement going from the old 'plusses' to the junior 'plusses'.

'Middle-men' and the transfer of knowledge

However, when two societies meet to exchange their material or cultural goods, the linear pattern is broken by the appearance of indispensable 'middle-men'.

The members of the élite in the developed society are, *ipso facto*, also the element most deeply rooted in their own milieu, and they do not usually leave their country and establish themselves abroad in a society with a different level of culture or development. The case of Dr Albert Schweitzer, the scientist, musician and theologian, who left Europe for Gabon, is the exception. So is the case of the Jews from Germany, who went to Palestine or elsewhere in considerable numbers, despite being deeply rooted in their country, because the alternative was extermination. In fact, many of them were so embedded in German life and culture that not even Nazism was sufficient to persuade them to get out in time – and they were exterminated.

One can find many intelligent people among the millions of Europeans who have gone overseas, but very few 'embedded' ones. The number of the latter shrinks even further among those who went out to the colonies. Their motivation varied: some were dissatisfied people, at odds with themselves, with their society or with both; others were adventurers, seeking short-cuts to money, glory or God; some were young people in a hurry, going abroad in order to be able to integrate better and at a higher level in their home society, after their return. Clearly all these types cannot be put into one category, but they are visibly distinguishable from those people who, because they are or wish to become 'plusses', and because they are embedded in their own society, do not act, except in exceptional circumstances, as vehicles of transculturation. This role is left to the 'men-in-the-middle', who choose to fulfil this task usually because they are in some sense 'marginal' to their own societies.

If we mark these middle-men (again without attaching any value-judgement to the sign) with a minus sign (−), the diagram of culture transfer between integrated societies at different levels of development would be as follows:

Figure 1

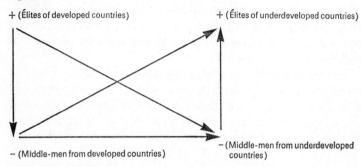

From this diagram we see that there can be one or more breaks in the transfer of culture from one society to another. We have one break in the case of the middle-man who acts as a direct link between the 'plusses' of the two societies. Such a man may either be an expatriate or an indigenous person; he may also belong to a third culture altogether. In the past, this type appeared so rarely that when successful the protagonist became famous. The Rothschild clan in Frankfurt, and the role they played between Britain and the Continent, could be cited as an example.

Recent social-anthropological researches in both western and non-western societies have shown that such phenomena are more common and extensive than was previously thought. Ronald Frankenburg studied the role of the 'stranger' in a Welsh village.[13] We also have C. P. Snow's discussion of foreign-born scientific advisers to the British military and political establishment (the Lindemann-Tizard controversy over Strategic Air Offensives during the Second World War, in *Science and Government*, 1961, and in *A Postscript to Science and Government*, 1962). Frankenberg states that in every group activity, it is possible to recognize

someone who has only that activity in common with the other members of the group, or is a deviant in some respect from the distinguishing criteria of the group mainly concerned. Such a person . . . is to some extent removed from the conflict and social pressures of full members of the group. This makes him or her of central importance in the precipitation and solution of such conflicts.[14]

In Africa it is very often the stranger who enforces on the community respect for central values, such as morality, care of property, food, the rules of exogamy, of burial, of ill omen, death, etc. This is sometimes achieved through the 'prescribed formula of joking which has been established as a standard relationship through the pattern of seemingly joking'.[15] Among the Allensi, it is within the next ring of clans – who are almost the enemy – that are to be found

the people who can exercise the strongest 'moral coercion' [Fortes] over you . . . hence, if a man gives up hope from grief and falls into despair, these are the people who urge him to rouse himself – and he cannot refuse lest ill from ancestral wrath afflict not only him but also all his line. These people are those on the very fringe of one's social relations, seemingly on the verge of moral relations.[16]

An opposite case would be that of an indigenous young man, such as Jomo Kenyatta, who, in the early thirties, after having spent long periods of his life acquiring education and experience abroad, is able to return home and maintain enough influence with his own traditionalist people to serve as an active vehicle of change and innovation. In Africa one does not have to search for such an exceptional case to discover a process of 'modernization from within' of this type. To quote Gluckman again,

legitimation of innovation does not necessarily come from the traditional authority. It can be drawn from any accepted indigenous authority – which can even be in opposition to the traditional one. The case of the Seventh Day Christians on the Tonga Plateau of Masabuka District in Northern Rhodesia corroborates this assumption. There seems to be a direct link between the Tonga's adhesion to this Christian sect and the fact that some of them became farmers in a country where the majority of the population were not. It is the result, *inter alia*, of the fact that they refuse to work on Saturday and thus cannot be employed as labourers in the European farms of the region. More important, the mission shows a much greater willingness than the Roman Catholics to accept *aliens* into schools and communities. The resulting interaction, plus the professional training some of its adherents obtain in Southern Rhodesia, produce a wider mental outlook. Here we may note that the big N'Debele growers, in the Mujinga Settlement . . . are also Seventh Day Adventists . . . These N'Debele have also set an example to their co-religionists.[17]

The status of the stranger

Let us assume that the process of transculturation is generally carried out through a series of middle-men of varying degrees of importance, with a comparable series of breaks in the process itself. Let us also assume that, as we have schematically shown, the transfer of know-how goes from the embedded 'plusses' of the donor society, through a number of 'minuses' (expatriate and/or indigenous middle-men) to the embedded 'plusses' of the recipient society. It then seems legitimate to ask whether and to what extent the man-in-the-middle can add or subtract something of his own to the message he is carrying from one society to another (thus becoming a promoter of, or an obstacle to, change) by virtue of his 'strangeness'.

In his analysis of the stranger, Alfred Schutz[18] defines him as 'an adult individual of our time and civilization who tries to be permanently accepted or at least tolerated by the group which he approaches'. For Shutz, the stranger is somebody who questions almost everything which appears unquestionable to the members of the group approached, because to him 'the cultural pattern of the approached group does not have the authority of attested system of recipes. And this, if for no other reason, because he does not partake in the vivid historical tradition by which it has been formed.' Insofar as he elicits attention, he also arouses questions and doubts which interrupt 'the flow of habit' and give rise 'to changed conditions of consciousness'.[19]

The stranger is also a man who has to face the fact that he lacks any status as a member of the social group he is about to join and is therefore unable to find a starting-point from which to take his bearings. He finds himself a border case outside the territory covered by the scheme of orientation current within the group.[20]

Seen from the outside, the cultural pattern of the group that the stranger wishes to approach, has nothing of the unity seen by the members of the in-group. A constant effort of 'translation' is thus required between the two. The stranger obviously cannot maintain this effort towards the whole group, but only towards a number of individuals who may be inclined to come into closer contact with him because they themselves are subject to a crisis in the 'thinking-as-usual' of the group.

To the stranger the observed actors within the approached group are not – as for their co-actors – of a certain presupposed anonymity, namely, mere performers of typical functions, but individuals . . . He is inclined to take mere individual traits as typical ones. Thus he constructs a social world of pseudo-anonymity, pseudo-intimacy and pseudo-typicality.[21]

All this contributes to the stranger's marginality, a situation which, at different levels of consciousness, is shared by every man-in-the-middle involved in the process of transculturation.

It is not the function of this study to discuss the pattern of marginality in society at large: for our purposes it will be sufficient if we consider as 'marginal men' those individuals who fit into G. Simmel's interpretation of the role of the stranger as a vehicle of culture and change.[22]

'Strangers' and 'foreigners'
The main idea presented by Simmel in this connection is that the marginality of the stranger is that of 'the man who came yesterday and stays tomorrow', as opposed to other outsiders who 'come today and go away tomorrow'. These latter could be called 'foreigners', not only because they remain separate from the society in which they operate (while the stranger is simultaneously in and out of the same society) but because they act on entirely different premises from those which motivate the stranger. The foreigner may be the conqueror, the colonizer, even the man who regards himself as superior by virtue of the message he carries, or the status he enjoys, or the power he possesses, but his role, his function, is nonetheless transient.

The force by which the foreigner maintains his position (temporarily) does not, of course, always mean physical force alone. A man can be a foreigner in a society by virtue of his faith or of his scientific power. And by thus being a foreigner he dooms himself to remain a transient element. If he insists on his distinctive element of separation, he is also doomed to lose it sooner or later. If he voluntarily renounces the elements of force which distinguish him from the rest of the society, he is quickly absorbed by that society. Indeed, all foreigners are in constant fear of being absorbed into the 'inferior' local population.

The foreigner, then, is a 'migrant bird', in contrast to Simmel's stranger, who 'came yesterday and stays tomorrow'. Strangers and foreigners are, by definition, marginal to the society in which they live. The prototype of the stranger is the trader, whether in goods, in ideas, or in both; the prototype of the foreigner is the expatriate colonial official. Traders must be strangers in order to make a living, since their job is to link those who are 'inside' with those who are 'outside'. Their force lies in their powers of persuasion, in their objectivity, which, as Simmel emphasizes, 'does not have to involve passivity or detachment'.

Strangers thus live and thrive in a situation of distance *and* proximity, of differences from *and* involvement with the communities between which they act as a bridge. This situation is quite different from the intellectual isolation which the Greeks wanted to maintain *vis-à-vis* the Barbarians, or the estrangement of those African tribes who traded with one another without ever exchanging a word. Foreigners, on the other hand, may be deeply involved in the affairs of the society in which they live, but they remain fundamentally detached from it, and linked with the country from which they come and from which they often continue to draw their power. When the foreigner's role is institutionalized, as in the case of diplomats, very special prerogatives are extended to them – such as the fiction whereby they continue to live 'abroad' through the right of extra-territoriality – to allow them to act as 'official foreigners'. Anyone who has seen a Gothic church built by British missionaries in East Africa for the benefit of native Christians, can feel how the 'estrangement' of a foreigner can express itself even through the religious style of a faith which calls for universal brotherhood among all the children of God.

The definition of a foreigner has intrigued jurists since the earliest times. So much so that two large volumes have recently been published on the subject by a learned society in Belgium, the Jean Bodin Society.[23]

In ancient Greece one finds the *Metoikos* (etymologically 'the one who lives with') and the *Xenoi* ('the one who stands without the community'). In Rome, the two groups were known as the *peregrinus* and the *barbarus*. In Ancient Mesopotamia, the stranger, as opposed to the foreigner, belonged to a social group called *Muskenu* (Mesquin, poor) meaning the men from the outside who established themselves within the Empire and enjoyed certain rights which were not extended to the foreigners.[24] In Hebrew the distinction is between *Ger* and *Nochri* – *Nochri* meaning the foreigner and *Ger* the 'other' who is part of the community.

More about strangers and foreigners
It is only recently that a functional definition of the stranger has been attempted. It was much easier to define foreigner, as opposed to stranger, functionally in a static society (static at least in intention, but also with few rapid changes) in which traditional values were known and defined and interpreted by traditional authority. It was easier, that is, than in a society dominated by the idea of rapid change and development, in which the position and the role (i.e. the function) of the men-in-the-middle (as well as that of the communication system) become the unstable yet central, critical part of the development process itself.

The functional distinction between foreigners and strangers becomes relevant to the problem of transculturation. As has already been stated, and contrary to what happens in integrated societies, the transfer of ideas and of know-how cannot take place between societies at different levels of development directly between the élites of both societies, without intermediaries. It must go through middle-men, since members of these societies do not usually meet, or co-opt each other. The existence of these middle-men breaks the normal or direct process of acculturation – the routine transfer of knowledge and authority from the élites of the older generation to the élites of the younger generation inside a society. The people who choose to act as middle-men between different societies and cultures are usually those who wish to act as 'keeper of the gate', and thus to choose a situation of marginality towards the societies which they connect. Their marginality may well derive from the fact that they are dissatisfied either with themselves or with what they are doing, or with their own societies, or with everything altogether.

But this state of dissatisfaction is not necessarily a negative element in society. The contrary has repeatedly been claimed, in particular in the field of scientific innovation, where the expression 'hybrid roles' has been coined to indicate those roles which have been chosen by persons (such as Freud and Pasteur, according to Ben-David)[25] who felt 'marginal' to and dissatisfied with the academic milieu in which they operated. This, however, was an intellectual, scientific marginality, not a social one, and whether it is at all relevant to our discussion need not be settled here.

The foreigner, who brings with him his own values and his own terms of reference, sticks to them – as long as he remains a foreigner – often with a passionate attachment bordering on the absurd. The sacramental character attached by European expatriates in the old colonial times to certain home customs, such as ceremonial dressing for dinner, the etiquette of sports and church-going, often in total disregard of local climatic or social conditions, is one of the central themes of colonial literature.

The ambiguity of the middle-man

The stranger, on the other hand, always fluctuates, because of his role as man-in-the-middle, and because of his tendency (in many, but not in all cases) to feel marginal to his own and to his adopted society, because of his oscillation between remoteness and intimacy, his hesitation and his uncertainty. In Schutz's words: 'the cultural pattern of the approached group is to the stranger not a shelter but a field of adventure'.[26] This explains why – as I have tried to show in a later chapter – adventurers, apart from their economic motives, were so attracted by the role of carriers of innovation (i.e. of men-in-the-middle) in Madagascar and elsewhere. But at the same time it also explains why they so often betrayed their masters and turned into foreigners. In fact, the two basic traits of the stranger's attitude towards the group with which he wants to come in contact are his objectivity (which favours his role as man-in-the-middle) and his doubtful loyalty (which hampers it). For Schutz, the stranger's deeper reason for objectivity lies in his own bitter experience which has taught him that a man-in-the-middle may lose his status and fortune from one moment to the next, and that his 'normal way of life' is always less secure than it seems.

For Simmel, the stranger's objectivity lies in his less than total commitment to the group, and this situation has two important consequences, at least for the promotion of innovation by the stranger himself. One is his ability to receive, because of his objectivity, 'the most surprising openness – confidences which sometimes have the character of a confession and which would be carefully withheld from a more related person'. The second is the stranger's freedom, insofar as the 'objective individual is bound by no commitments which could prejudice his perception, understanding and evaluation of the given'.

It is, in fact, from this situation of objectivity that the doubtful loyalty of the stranger stems. His permanent oscillation between two patterns of group life allows him to switch easily from the role of stranger, carrier of acceptable changes and innovation, to the role of foreigner, carrier of unacceptable changes and innovation. The reciprocal recriminations which accompany these shifts in loyalties stem from the astonishment of the members of the in-group that the stranger does not accept the totality of its cultural pattern as the natural and appropriate way of life. The stranger, on the other hand, is surprised that the in-group members do not perceive the fact that their pattern of life is not a protective shelter for him but a labyrinth in which he has lost his bearings. Simmel thinks that the very freedom enjoyed by the stranger is a further source of trouble. It is a freedom which allows the stranger to experience and to regard even his close relationships as if with a bird's-eye-view. And because he is freer, because he is not tied down in his actions by habit, piety and precedent, he is also liable to be the first victim of any uprising in which the party attacked claims that provocation has come from outside, through emissaries and instigators.

All this fits situations in which the stranger, acting as keeper of the gate, operates among slowly changing societies. But in an age dominated by the idea of, and the urge towards progress, development and change, the man-in-the-middle, by the mere fact of becoming a dynamic channel of intercommunication between multiple aspects of social, intellectual, economic and political life, all reciprocally influencing each other, turns into a powerful motor of the whole system, with an uncontrollable drive of his own. The situational logic according to which the keeper of the gate operates, often becomes the prevailing, even if unaccepted, logic of the system as a whole, thus transforming (sometimes with some justice) the impartiality of the stranger into the partiality of the foreigner.

Foreign educational systems

This is particularly true in the field of education and teaching. Quantitatively, the increase of education in underdeveloped countries is phenomenal and, as the Pearson Report notes, enrolments in the developing countries studied by the Commission tripled between 1950 and 1965. This enlarged the horizons of millions of people, while the presence of increasing numbers of educated people has 'immeasurably' influenced the organization of their societies.

Unfortunately, disconcerting phenomena appeared simultaneously: there has been a 70 per cent drop-out in primary schools; at university level, most students started courses in law and political sciences, or in the traditional fields of engineering, but only a small fraction ever graduated. 'In too many instances,' says the Report, 'children who finish primary schools in rural areas seem rather less fit to become creative and constructive members of their own community than if they had never been at school.'

To attribute much of the responsibility for this set-back, as the Pearson Report rightly does, to the inadequacy of the curricula and systems inherited from colonial days, is to admit – willy nilly – the foreignness of such systems. But to ignore the fact – pointed out by many students of educational problems, particularly in Africa [27] – that many underdeveloped countries have stubbornly refused to change these curricula because they fear that a system of education based on African (or Indian, or Indonesian) needs might be a device aimed at preventing equality between African and European, means evading a recognition of the distorted, foreign and psychologically perverted view of themselves which imported education and foreign-trained educators have given to the 'educated' people in underdeveloped countries. This is a view which the keepers of the gate really do control, and for which they must be held responsible.

Whatever their view of the world, of society, and of their origins, and irrespective of the fact that, as teachers, they may set an example of authoritarianism, of contempt for rural life, or of personal frustration (at not having achieved a higher professional rank through education), the basic fact remains that through their teaching of subjects and methods which have been imported from outside and not elaborated in the local society, they represent a world and ideals which are generally foreign to the local and family environment in which their pupils belong. 'One reason,' says Williams, 'why it is so difficult to use education to transform society and the economy, is precisely that teachers are so often not the pacemakers in social progress.' [28]

One suggested remedy [29] has been the conversion of the whole teaching profession from the teaching of facts to an encouragement of inquiry and understanding. (This is a process, incidentally, which could do a lot of good for the educational systems of developed countries.)

More on micro-cooperation
The appropriate educational approach, I venture to suggest, should be the promotion of techniques of activating men towards change in their own setting, as well as activating the traditional élites towards providing an accepted legitimization of the new, by an appropriate reinterpretation of the past. This is, in my view, one of the tasks of what I call *micro-cooperation*, an example of which will be described in detail in chapter V, with reference to the Israeli occupation of the West Bank of the River Jordan. At this point I only wish to state my belief that one way of introducing change is to have it legitimized by the traditional authorities. In traditional societies, only legitimate authority can innovate without running the risk of transforming the indispensable strangers – the carriers of innovation – into foreigners who will provoke persistent and often irrational opposition.

Due to the dynamic role played by the stranger – indigenous or expatriate – as the carrier of innovation in societies which submit, willingly or unwillingly, to the influence of the call of progress, it becomes very difficult for the modern technical adviser, or any keeper of the gate, to rely only on persuasion and remain completely impartial, as a stranger should. The appeal to force, especially when its use appears justified by the benefits which innovation and change can bring to a traditionalist society, becomes irresistible. And with it comes the identification of the man-in-the-middle (expatriate or indigenous) with that very element of coercion – educational, political, technological or industrial –

which makes him a foreigner, a transient, and therefore of little value to the process of transculturation.

The capacity of a society to develop and change is influenced by the aid it receives and/or the number of people employed in the transculturation process. It is also a function of the society's ability to transform foreigners into strangers, and to allow strangers to act as vehicles of transculturation, quite independently of the personal idiosyncrasies of the man-in-the-middle himself. This ability seems to depend to a very large extent on the direction in which the 'imitative hold' of the traditional élite is exerted over the 'vehicles' of transculturation active in a given society. This, in turn, changes according to the type of authority which the élite possesses: it may be a political authority, as distinct from social, cultural, religious and economic authority, or a combination of these.[30]

The political setting for micro-cooperation
In a developed as well as in a non-developed society, there may exist a dichotomy of interest, views or ideas between the governing and the non-governing élites. Such a dichotomy does not necessarily mean that the influence of the people with governmental authority and of those who have non-governmental authority always move in divergent directions. On the other hand, an identity of aspirations between governing and non-governing influential groups does not necessarily mean that their imitative hold over the masses is exercised in the same direction.[31]

The direction and extent of an imitative hold may, in fact, have little to do with political ideas and political power – though the fact of power is always a very important element in the creation and perpetuation of the imitative hold. Thus, there could be several possible combinations of the imitative hold of governing and non-governing élites, or – to use current sociological terminology – of *primary* and *secondary* élites.

A governing (primary) and a non-governing (secondary) élite may exercise an imitative hold in the same direction. This usually happens in the case of integrated societies in which both the bodies share a common basis of cultural, religious, social, economic, and possibly political beliefs and aspirations. Most western societies – including the communist ones – are of this kind. So must have been, for instance, many pre-colonial non-western societies, such as pre-colonial Madagascar.

But what happens when the holders of governing power and the holders of non-governing influence disagree on the method to be used to achieve common goals, to the point where they come to an open clash? In a developed society the clash may not be of decisive importance *for the process of development*, since the primary, governing élite is only one of the élites involved in the process itself. But in a developing country, in which the governing élite – whether indigenous or expatriate – usually monopolizes most of the country's resources, the clash can have considerable consequences, in spite of the fact that the governmental and non-governmental leaders share the same basic aspirations.

In the case of a primary élite which exercises its imitative hold in a direction different from that of the secondary élite, we are theoretically faced with three possibilities: (a) that the primary governing élite's imitative hold is stronger than that of the secondary non-governing élite; (b) that the opposite is the case, and (c) that they are equal in strength. In fact, however, I know of no examples of the third possibility.

Typical examples of the first possibility are the expatriate communities of Africa, such as the British in Kenya or the French in Senegal. In colonial times both the political and social authority of the expatriate élites, and their imitative hold, remained supreme. The logic of the direct colonial ruling system demanded that the colonial rule dispose first of all of those indigenous governing or non-governing élites which might offer effective resistance to the establishment of the colonial rule.[32] Further, in some colonial territories (more in the case of French, Belgian and Italian colonial administrations than those of the British, at least in territories like Buganda or Northern Nigeria, where the principle of indirect rule has been followed more than elsewhere) the need of the administration for low-ranking clerical and military manpower led to the social and administrative promotion to the top of those indigenous elements which most readily accepted foreign domination. Their advancement was promoted by an educational system run by the missionaries and by the lay administrative and military recruiting systems – i.e. by foreigners. All these foreign bodies selected their candidates from the most submissive social and ethnic groups of the country concerned (the sons of the slaves, the members of lower castes, paupers, etc.) because these were obviously the people who were more ready to cooperate with the conquerors. The members of the indigenous upper class kept away from, or were denied the advantages of educational or administrative association with the new expatriate rulers, at least in the first stages of colonization.

In due course, as a result of economic, administrative and educational advancement, the low-caste indigenous elements serving the direct colonial ruler, were transformed into an indigenous élite. Often they became more powerful than the old, traditional, pre-colonial élite. They acquired cultural and social (though not necessarily political) aspirations similar to those of the governing expatriate élite – that is, the ruling foreigners – to which this new indigenous élite owed its status and success, and to which it was naturally attracted.[33]

Since in colonial society, to be successful largely meant to look and to act like an expatriate, the new indigenous, non-governing élite – the priest, the schoolteacher, the chief clerk, the judge, the successful merchant, the physician – increasingly adopted the way of life of the ruling expatriates, in order to join the élite. They continued to maintain these habits even after achieving political independence, when they themselves became the governing élite. Their imitative hold over the traditionalist masses remained weak, and was further weakened by a resurgence of tribal influence, and by the competition with the traditional chiefs for control of the same popular basic sources of authority, mentioned before. In fact, one of the main differences between the old colonial and the new indigenous rulers in Africa is that the authority of the former extended over the inhabitants of a whole territory, irrespective of tribal differences, and drew its force and legitimacy from abroad. By contrast, the new, native, governing leadership often finds its influence restricted to its own ethnic group, and has to draw legitimation from the same sources as other indigenous competing élites. Only rarely is an indigenous leader able to develop a nation-wide, non-political imitative hold which extends to all ethnic groups. Thus, paradoxically, even after independence, the influence of the former colonial governing élite often remains stronger than that of the indigenous governing and non-governing élites.

There are, however, cases in which the second situation exists – namely, where the imitative hold of the indigenous non-governing élite remains superior to, and divergent from that of the governing élite. The case of Mandatory Palestine is an example of this – admittedly a very special one.

In Mandatory Palestine, the governing élite was expatriate and British, the non-governing élites were Jewish and Arab. The imitative hold of the Jewish non-governing élite was extremely powerful in social and educational spheres, but weak in the field of politics. The Jews never imitated the British way of life: they organized a society of their own, based on collective and cooperative structures, on values and symbols which remained, by and large, impervious to British influence. When, for instance, the British tried to use the schools in order to influence the education of the future élites of the Jewish community, the Jews renounced their right to use tax revenue for education, and voluntarily raised an extra tax among themselves to support an independent school system. On the other hand, in the political sphere, the British unintentionally ruled the day: although most of the Jews came from non-democratic and non-English-speaking countries, they adopted the British judicial system, and developed British habits of information and democratic practices.

The reaction of the Arabs was very different. With them the British imitative hold was strong in social matters. To this very day the Palestinian upper class in Jordan makes extensive use of the English language; Jordanian television uses the same publicity stereotypes for commercials – sexy British girls and distinguished British gentlemen. British army uniforms, British sports, British standards of education, are still in full use. When the Israelis occuped the West Bank of the Jordan they were surprised to find the local Arab administration using the same files and forms as were in use twenty years earlier, under the Mandatory Government.

Political power and behaviour in Jordan, on the other hand, have remained quite untouched by British tradition, certainly as far as freedom of the press and independence of Parliament are concerned. This situation can, of course, be attributed not only to the reciprocal relations between primary and secondary élites, but to the ability of the élites themselves to remain more or less 'open' in their status and social perceptions.

S. N. Eisenstadt has discussed this problem in another context, dealing with the relations between modernization and Protestant ethics. Some of his observations are relevant to the topics under discussion here. 'On the level of the development of new roles and organizations' – he writes – 'more than in the case of development of new motivations . . . characteristics of the *broader institutional* setting of the societies in which these movements take place may be of great importance in facilitating or impeding the institutionalization of their transformative potentials.' [34] It is quite evident that in the case of the Palestinian Arabs who remained under Jordanian rule, the 'broader institutional settings' remained beyond the influence of the western world – in spite of the apparent sympathy shown by Arab élites in Jordan for the 'British way of life' – whereas the 'broader institutional settings' of the Israelis coincided fairly well with those of the western world, in spite of social and political tension with the British in the latter part of their Mandatory rule over Palestine.

There is little doubt that the rapidity of modernization in Israel was due to the fact that, when the Jewish non-governing leaders of colonial Palestine took over the responsibilities of power, they carried with them a genuine imitative hold of their own. On the other hand, they had to adopt foreign patterns in matters such as protocol, parliamentary procedure, and – in the first years of independence – army organization (an organization, incidentally, which was responsible for much of the military weakness of the army between 1949 and 1954). Following the appointment of General Dayan as Chief-of-Staff, however, the whole structure of the army was changed to a basis of local 'Israeli' principles, breaking away from all imported British Army traditions and systems. [35] This facilitated the assimilation of the many changes later introduced into the Jewish society, and the diffusion of the aid-to-development which the Israeli government was able to mobilize, which was – and still is – the main adult educational organization of the Israeli society.

Summary

Let me recapitulate: I have claimed that the process of transculturation is, by definition, carried out by a man-in-the-middle, who can fulfil his functions as a vehicle of change either in the role of a stranger or of a foreigner.

Assuming this, I would suggest that if the man-in-the-middle acts as a stranger, the success of his efforts at modernization will depend to a considerable extent on his ability to obtain legitimation for his innovation from the traditional authority in the field of innovation itself.

If, on the other hand, the man-in-the-middle acts as a foreigner, it seems that he must be able to muster sufficient power for an adequate period of time, in order to be able to impose himself and his new ideas and values upon the recipient society. This is very difficult to achieve, even in the narrow sphere of a specific technical change, when the sources of this indispensable legitimacy are different for the promoter and the recipient of the innovation.

It is claimed that the imitative process by which an innovation can spread – especially when the diffusion of innovation is intentional, as in the case of aid-to-development – is infinitely more difficult to elicit when the change is introduced by someone acting (or considered to be acting) as a foreigner, than it would be if introduced by someone accepted as a stranger. This holds true even if the 'goods' offered by the former person are superior to those of the latter. Anyone who has been in French- or English-speaking Africa knows of the magnificent agricultural stations built up by colonial experts for the purpose of promoting modernization in the native agriculture. As research stations for the European experts, and for the advancement of science, they are undisputed successes; but as channels of modernization they are monumental failures, since they usually remain surrounded, after years of operation, by the most primitive native farms, which have remained absolutely untouched by the foreign example.

However, to illustrate the above claim – and the claim that micro-cooperation is a suitable technique in aid-to-development – at least two further points have to be made. First, up till now much of the process of transculturation from western to non-western was carried out by non-indigenous agents operating in a traditional society; the ability of these agents to perform their role of active carriers of innovation was small, as they were strangers; it further decreased when their status changed – in the eyes of the recipient society – from stranger to foreigner. Second, if the planners of development employ appropriate techniques of micro-cooperation – even when there is diffused opposition to imported changes – traditional authority can be activated and harnessed to the process of development. These points will be taken up in the two following chapters.

Chapter 4

Micro-Cooperation
Ancient and Modern

Three Case Studies

In 1964 an Israeli expert in cooperative organization was sent by his government to Madagascar at the request of the local ruling socialist party to advise on the setting up of cooperatives in the rural district south of Tananarive, the capital. He was struck by the success of a European entrepreneur who had organized in a village a semi-cooperative production of hand-woven tissues from raffia. When he suggested a detailed plan for expanding this branch of trade, however, he met with much official opposition. The scheme, he was told, could work only if some non-monetary incentive could be found to compensate the cooperative workers. The people engaged in the 'private cooperative' had indeed done very well and had considerably increased their income. But they had also spent all their savings, not on improving their standard of living, but building or enlarging their family tombs. It was clearly more important for them, both from the religious and status standpoints, to provide better 'accommodation' for the dead than for the living, who would, in any case, dwell in their homes only for a limited number of years. Furthermore, the new tomb-building activity of the raffia weavers had aroused jealousy and competition among the inhabitants of the same village who had not been included in the raffia production scheme. Loans had been taken at very high interest rates by these people, in order not to lose status. This indicated that if the raffia weaving cooperative project had to be carried out, alternative social and economic incentives – other than the purely monetary ones offered by the private entrepreneur – had to be thought out, in order not to create an additional burden on an already weak regional economy through what appeared to be a perfectly logical and promising development initiative.

The diaries of technical advisers the world over are full of this kind of story, which make the subject of small talk at all diplomatic cocktail parties in every capital city of underdeveloped countries. To recall them would not only be banal, after the success of books like *The Ugly American* or *The Ugly Russian*, it would also be unfair. Ugly or not, what makes a technical adviser ugly or handsome – in terms of the aid-to-development job he has to carry out – is not his character, nor his political ideas, nor his personal charm, not even his personal success or failure in dealing with people. It is his ability to help people to help themselves, and not just to help them (or not to help them) directly.

The ability to activate the will to develop in a certain direction among members of a different society, the aptitude to cause an innovation to be adopted and diffused independently of the continued presence of the innovator himself – these are the vital factors in all types of aid-to-development, which no macro-cooperation scheme can hope to achieve, even if it is successful in realizing major planned environmental changes.

'A jungle remains a jungle, whether it is a Communist or a capitalist jungle,' says John Kenneth Galbraith. This is true not only in the objective physical sense, but also in the somewhat less objective sociological and cultural sense. A society is a 'jungle' of institutionalized beliefs, prejudices, metaphysical concepts, perceptions, interdependent cultural approaches, etc., as well as a jungle of institutions and bureaucracies, all of which are interconnected: they cannot be changed at one point without thereby changing elsewhere. This truth is well known to any ecologist.

The internal balance of a society can certainly be changed in favour of development and modernization. The inborn resistance to innovation, it has by now been realized, is quite a myth, notwithstanding the fact that it has been amply validated through the experience of two decades of aid-to-development efforts; it is still a myth. What is also clear, however, is that men resent being changed by a pushing alien, by outside pressure. The important element in imported change, then, if it is to succeed, is to set it in motion in such a way that it may easily be picked up by some members of the community, and from then on treated as indigenous. Insofar as the innovation is a known import item, it may be important for its successful transplantation that the members of the community who pick it up be members of the indigenous élite which can legitimize the adoption of the known import item and thus foster its diffusion in the community.

In the previous chapter I have attempted to show that the status of the carrier of innovations can be polarized between the status of a foreigner (the visitor) and that of a stranger (the newcomer), the former generally being a poor carrier of innovation, while the latter is an indispensable element in the process of transplantation. Between these two poles, need one say, many intermediate positions can be taken up by the carrier of innovation, who can also move backwards and forwards between the two extremes under the pressure of changing circumstances – circumstances which he himself may well have set in motion. The roles of the stranger and of the foreigner, therefore, are fluid and not fixed within the frame of that system of micro-cooperation which we consider essential to the success of any programme of aid-to-development.

In this chapter I shall try to discuss the process of shift between the two roles, and even the possible total switch from one to the other. I shall try to do this with the help of three examples, taken from widely differing types of underdeveloped societies exposed to impacts of modernization. I shall concentrate on three cases: first the role of the foreigner/stranger in a pre-colonial society, nineteenth-century Madagascar, and then in two contemporary societies, Afghanistan and Peru. Let me explain my choice. While other relevant and modern cases might easily have been found to illustrate my claim that innovation takes better when legitimized by local élites, I chose the case of nineteenth-century Madagascar. It is, first of all, the only known case of an indigenous effort at westernization and industrialization of an African country (or at least a country close to Africa) in the first part of the nineteenth century. It is also the only case known to us in which written records have been preserved in both European (French and English) and local (the Malagasy) languages, records which can be counterchecked to a very large extent against the rich evidence accumulated outside Madagascar.[1] The various trends and points of view involved in this process of modernization can thus be compared.

The Malagasy experience seems unique because, on a very limited scale, it presents some similarities with the process of modernization of other non-European countries, such as China and Japan. But, contrary to what happened in both the latter countries, the final and catastrophic result in Madagascar allows us to look at an experience of modernization which completed its full cycle in less than three generations. The bits and pieces of this experience lay themselves open to investigation, not like a complete though unusable instrument, but like the scattered parts of a broken machine. I was fascinated by all this when I first read about it, and I have tried elsewhere to describe how this machine worked.[2] Here, I shall focus on one of its elemental 'cogs' only – the European carriers of innovation.

In the second part of this chapter I shall attempt to look at the same element, this time in the form of members of the American Peace Corps, operating in contemporary underdeveloped societies – Afghanistan and Peru. It has been claimed that the one was a failure and the other a success. This is why I chose them.

I. THE MADAGASCAR CASE

a. *The Historical Setting*
In the wake of the Napoleonic Wars, the British occupied Isle de France, which reverted to its old name of Mauritius,[3] while the nearby island of Bourbon (La Réunion) was returned to the French.

For both islets, densely inhabited by a slave population and a strong white and creole French colonial upper class, the natural area of expansion was the nearby island-continent of Madagascar.

Under the energetic leadership of Sir Robert Farquhar, the first British Governor of Mauritius, the French (who for two centuries had tried to establish themselves on the southern coast of Madagascar) were successfully kept out of the Great Island. Farquhar managed this by helping one of the chieftains – the modernizing king of the Hovas – to reinforce his military power and unify the whole country under his kingship. This was one of the first comprehensive programmes of modernization ever initiated by a

European country – at least in Africa – and it was carried out with considerable success from 1813 to 1835 by a very small group of British military and diplomatic advisers (three or four) and by a dozen or so missionaries and their families. Following the death of Radama I and the accession to the throne of his wife, Queen Ranavalona I, in 1826, the social and political problems connected with the process of imported modernization became one of the main foci of internal tension in the Hova society. The British advisers and missionaries were gradually expelled, the country assumed complete isolation, and a group of European adventurers, mainly French but also some Greek and American, were invited to take over from the missionaries and to carry on with the policy of autarchic modernization, mainly to provide for the needs of the indigenous army of the local aristocracy. Again, they were most successful in their enterprises, especially in those initiated and organized by a French adventurer, Jean Laborde. But the whole process again came to an abrupt stop in 1857, after the failure of an attempt by some Europeans to overthrow the Queen in favour of her son, Radama II, a converted Christian and a partisan of a radical policy of westernization and cooperation with Europe, and with France in particular. He eventually inherited the Malagasy throne after the Queen's death in 1860, but was murdered two years later by the most extreme conservative and anti-European elements in the capital.

These political and social upheavals were accompanied by recurrent waves of persecution of Christian converts, who were detested by the régime, not so much for their new religion as because their faith identified them with the modernizing party which was supposed to be under the direct influence of the 'foreigners beyond the sea'.

Thus, we see in the highlands of Madagascar – or Imerina – from 1820 to 1860, all the elements – albeit in embryo – of a modernization drama like in most non-European underdeveloped countries exposed to a sudden strong impact of westernization: imported development versus traditional backwardness; private initiative versus government-controlled modernization; mass modern education versus indigenous cultural tradition; technical assistance versus tribal anarchy and xenophobia; new social and religious values versus old traditions and myths; diplomatic intrigues versus dispassionate self-sacrifice; hope for rapid development versus frustration caused by slow advance.

b. *The 'Carriers' of Modernization in Pre-Colonial Madagascar*

One can distinguish four main groups involved in the process of transculturation in pre-colonial Madagascar: the missionaries; the Malagasy élite; the official political and military advisers; and the expatriate adventurers.

The Missionaries
The missionaries were a very small group, seldom more than half a dozen men at any one time (say twenty souls, including their wives and children), yet they achieved extraordinary results.[4] They transcribed the Malagasy language into Latin characters, organized a vast native educational system, over which they presided, involving about 10,000 pupils; they introduced the idea of Christianity more widely and more deeply than the actual number of conversions might imply; they brought with them 'mechanics', the artisans who introduced many basic trades into the island – printing, shoemaking, tanning, weaving, ironmongery, carpentry, building, toolmaking, and so on. Some of these 'mechanics' showed extraordinary energy and genius. One such was James Cameron[5] who built the first palace for the Queen, created a number of workshops, trained hundreds of native artisans, taught chemistry and mathematics at school, and acted as a kind of Robinson Crusoe on an island thickly inhabited by industrious Man Fridays.

The missionaries who went to Madagascar – and elsewhere – were all deeply convinced of the superiority of their Christian faith: they were ready to die for it, and often did so. However, their faith also had a political aspect not only because it aimed at keeping the French Catholics out of Madagascar, but because it was part and parcel of a British way of life which they regarded as being culturally and socially higher than other cultures and societies, just as Protestantism to them was higher than other religions.

Once abroad, the British missionaries (in Madagascar and elsewhere)[6] formed a small group of people who made a point of living according to what they thought were the dignified standards of life of the British gentry; no easy matter in a far-away country, submitted to foreign rule, strong economic and power temptations, social pressures and constant community tensions.[7] The missionaries' diaries and correspondence (which can be counterchecked against documents from the Malagasy archives) show us how their work met with unexpected obstacles and how their actions were misunderstood by the natives, not because they pursued any given policy but just because their conduct was guided by values, habits and social codes, pertaining to a different society and culture.[8] Tied up in this strait-jacket, like so many of our contemporary technical advisers, the missionaries had to struggle with problems of status, faith, money, and their political and social relations with the native authorities – four problems which I would like to discuss in some detail.

The status problems of the missionaries were in most cases caused by their constant feeling of living at the periphery of their own and of the native society. They stood somewhat outside the British society in which they lived at home and into which many hoped to re-integrate (at a higher social level) upon their return, thanks to their missionary achievements overseas. On the other hand, when they did not die of fever or by the sword, missionaries tended to achieve a position of authority and wealth which was very different from the poverty and social inferiority they usually knew in England. We have British official diplomatic reports about their horses and houses, their wives' dresses and their slaves.[9] In Tananarive, the capital of the Hova Kingdom, the missionaries fought bitterly against the British Agent in order to maintain direct, and possibly more influential channels of communication with the native government.[10] Their pressure, *in loco* and at home, on the British authorities, to promote, protect and extend their religious activities in the country was persistent.[11] If one replaces the word 'Agency' with the word 'Embassy', and 'Mission' with 'Technical Aid Mission', one has in the Tananarive capital of 1820 many of the institutional problems and intrigues that are usually found today in any newly independent country's capital, where the representatives of the metropolitan Foreign Ministries jockey for influence and position with the representatives of the Cooperation Ministries, those of Defence Ministries with those of Economic Ministries, and so on.

All this is neither new nor surprising: what is interesting is that the Malagasy have left us written evidence of how they regarded these foreigners' squabbles – how they played the (aid) mission against the political mission, how rapidly they discovered the true social status of each and every missionary, how they used their complexes and their marginality as political cards to be played for the benefit of Malagasy national – or, more often – internal political interests.[12]

One could wish that we had similar official records of the attitudes of contemporary political leaders of underdeveloped countries to our foreign aid policies. All we have to rely on are the speculations of the experts on the donor side, who – like the missionaries of old – tend to divide the actions of those involved in aid-to-development into the schematized performances of 'good' and 'bad' Americans, Russians, Israelis, etc.

The second important point is the faith of the missionaries. Of the honesty and strength of their personal faith there is little doubt. With one possible exception, the missionary group which worked for over ten years in Madagascar gave outstanding proof of its high religious qualities. But not all of their religious activities had either a religious aim or religious consequences.

I have already suggested how important it was for the British Protestant clergymen to keep out Catholic priests with their French influence. Far more important was the political impact that Christian teaching had on the political life and structures of Malagasy society. By introducing printing into a country which had no written language and no transport system apart from human carriers, they introduced a new, powerful system of communication, which was so selective (since it could be used only by a small number of educated men) as to look like a 'secret code', or at least like the basic means of joining a powerful social and political 'club'.

The Christian message formed the main subject of what was printed and taught, together with grammar, arithmetic and trades. Textbooks for reading and writing the Malagasy language were based on biblical texts. Basic economic and social ideas, essential to modernization of a western type, such as trade, credit, free organization, democratic systems of decision by voting, etc., were constantly introduced through religious channels and with religious terminology. With these ideas came others: revolutionary, social and political ideas such as the equality of man, the dignity of the individual, the rights of the poor, the morality of a society based on private property, monogamy, and so on. To accept these ideas, and to elaborate on them, meant undercutting some of the political premises on which the traditional, tribal and aristocratic Malagasy society was based. It was no coincidence that the decision to expel the missionaries was taken soon after a Malagasy 'prophet' began to preach a new kind of native religion strongly tainted with Christian ideas. It was also not a coincidence that one of the first quarrels between the King and the missionaries was over the organization and running of the Missionary Schools Society founded in 1826.[13]

The Malagasy Élite

Turning to the second group, the Malagasy élite, we can easily see how much more impressed they were by the new political and social ideas brought in by the Europeans, than by their techniques.[14] Quite apart from the human, moral and social inspiration which the Malagasy – a deeply religious people – derived from Christianity, the new religion, which today would be called an 'ideology', served as a common denominator for people from different levels of society. This denominator, by cutting across the traditional strata, mixed old-established loyalties, provided the framework for new cooperation or common resistance among people who felt they had common interests to promote or defend. However, what was lacking and what the missionaries were unable to create, was a set of new institutions through which to express and coordinate these feelings. This was not because of their lack of authority (they organized a school system for thousands of pupils, and their mechanics were capable of building great factories or trade companies) but because they had no control over the sources of legitimization of the accepted authority. To be Christian or pro-Christian soon came to mean belonging to a party whose foundations were alien to the indigenous mind and society. Christianity became an idea to be fought against by the traditionalist elements in Madagascar, not for what it said about God, but for what it spurred men on to say about their leaders and their own rights.

Of the thousands of Malagasies who fell victim to the anti-

Christian persecutions which followed the expulsion of the missionaries, few were really Christians: they were upper-class people, army officers, merchants, officials, intellectuals, who had found in the new Christian faith and ideas a wider political framework for the expression of, and a justification for, their views and interests. They had thus become a danger to the traditional vested interests and élites in the country.[15]

If we substitute the words 'capitalism' or 'Marxism' for the word 'Christianity', the old quarrel between the Malagasy government and the missionaries takes on a modern form. 'You should give us the tools,' said the Malagasy government to the Europeans, 'and we will do the job.' To which the retort of the European missionaries was: 'The tools are part of western Christian civilization: without accepting its values, you cannot use its tools.'

Such an approach can be valid for societies like Japan, India or China, that can oppose the 'metaphysic' of the West with their own 'metaphysic', and the foreign culture with their own compact body of traditional learning. But when the meeting of two cultures takes the form of a clash between a highly developed culture and a very weak one, then the cohesion of the group which works with a sense of mission becomes all important, and this not only because of the combined energy it can develop, but also because of the choices it makes of subjects to be taught and those to be withheld.

In the case of Madagascar, the choices made by the Protestant missionaries were largely independent of the wishes and needs of the recipient party, since they – the 'giving' side – were passionately attached to the vision they had of their own values, and to their own appreciation of what was good or bad for the other side.

As for the young Malagasy sent to England to study, immediately upon his return home he was caught up in the dilemma of what he should teach. Quite apart from his resentment at being put under the supervision of foreigners (which sometimes created personal tension), he had to face the fact that he could not detach the tools from the ideas which produced them, even in simple things such as printing operations. (Where was he to find texts to translate and to print, if the only available ones were religious?)

He was supposed to inherit the white man's knowledge and pass it on to his fellow natives. In fact, because of the white man's suspect political position in Malagasy society, the only thing that the native trainee could do was to despise the values of a culture he could not master. Instead of being a source of even limited information, he became a source of faulty communication – or low entropy, as the cyberneticians would say. The foreign message which he was supposed to pass on became – even if correctly translated into the native language – distorted and unintelligible for his pupils, because he could not convey the values underlying the message. He used much of his newly acquired foreign knowledge to fight those people whose very presence represented a permanent witness to his lack of knowledge.[16]

The Military Advisers

The political and military advisers to the Malagasy were, on the whole, a far less complicated group. They had the advantage – unlike the missionaries – of belonging to institutions which possessed clear and defined aims, which exercised some sort of disciplinary control over them, if by no other means than through the regular payment of salaries. The interesting point about the British military advisers in Madagascar is that the most successful were those who came from low-ranking positions in the British military colonial establishment. In their dealings with the native aristocracy they found not only a challenge, the outcome of which could bring praise from their superiors, but also a true feeling of social promotion.

Brady, who rose to be a Marshal in the Malagasy army, was a mulatto drill sergeant from Jamaica. He found no difficulty in marrying into the Malagasy upper class.[17] James Hastie, who became the King's blood brother, his financial associate, and a great reformer of Malagasy society, was an Indian Army sergeant of Scottish extraction. He was undoubtedly a man of extraordinary moral and intellectual qualities. But in Mauritius, where he had been stationed, he was not allowed to sit down while reporting to General Hall, the Acting-Governor, on his mission to Tananarive. The colonial society of the time would not accept him as a gentleman, but only as a sergeant.[18]

To Hastie, the diplomatic mission to the King of Madagascar was not only a great intellectual challenge, but also a great social opportunity. He married a local princess, became very rich, and was so attached to Madagascar that he asked to be buried in his new home country. He was the perfect type of successful administrator and dispenser of technical aid: a man who knew how to adapt himself to the logic of the local situation. He was helped to do this by his realization that the native society could recognize his abilities better than his own society, and was ready to repay such recognition with devotion and understanding.

Robin, a French sergeant, probably a deserter from Napoleon's army, who arrived in Madagascar in 1819, was certainly not controlled by any institution but, starting from his NCO's rank, he became secretary to the King and his teacher of French and arithmetic. He played a large part in the organization of the Palace Officers' School and rose to the rank of Grand Marshal of the Palace in 1836.[19]

On the other hand, Hastie's successor as British Agent was Dr Robert Lyall, a gentleman, a scientist, and a man of established reputation in British society. When appointed to Madagascar, he tried to impress the King with his superior scientific knowledge – a 'magic' knowledge he could not share with the Malagasy. He gave to the role of British Resident a new image: that of a powerful foreign magician who could no longer be considered 'one of the family'. It was a different approach which implied a different style. Lyall was unable to part – as Hastie did – with the outward symbols of his official position; for instance, from his heavy red and gold uniform. Even in the greatest heat he took much pleasure in wearing it. He could not stand the sordid but humanly understandable business which some of the missionaries were engaged in, in order to make a living.[20] He could not admit that the Queen's orders should be transmitted to him through the senior churchman, even if this missionary's role of temporary adviser to the Queen might have been of some use to the Residency.[21] He stood on protocol – British protocol, naturally – on and off duty. He was, and remained to the end, a foreigner.

Thus ended the British political presence and protectorate in Madagascar.

The Adventurers
When Lyall was expelled in 1830, his place – and later (1835) the place of the British missionaries also – was taken by a band of

mainly French adventurers, who did not represent any foreign government, but were a useful means of communication with the outer world. The most famous of these adventurers was Jean Baptiste Laborde. Another was M. de Lestelle.[22] The group was asked, or rather allowed by the Malagasy to continue the process of modernization started by the British, but on condition that they work in total isolation from the outside world, and in close association with the Malagasy.

Their services were required primarily to provide a modern infra-structure to support the military establishment. To this end Laborde created gun factories and steel mills, workshops for the repair of all kinds of weapons, and laboratories for the preparation of gunpowder and primers. However, in the process he and his associates also created factories for the production of non-military goods, such as bricks, furniture, hats, chocolates, lightning rods, and soap. They worked exclusively to satisfy the requirements of the Queen, her court and the plutocratic élite of the capital. They operated on lavish grants and concessions with unlimited forced labour conscripted by the government. Out of their activities came the first chemical products of Madagascar – for instance, sulphuric acid (obtained by soaking animal bowels in buckets of urine, which the citizens of the capital had to provide and carry to the factory). Laborde managed to smelt iron and produce potash; he imported steam machinery from Europe and merino sheep from Australia; he developed vineyards and zoological gardens, built aqueducts, dams and palaces, and organized night banquets with fireworks, in imitation of those at Versailles. He acted as a member of the Malagasy upper class, on whom the Queen bestowed Malagasy honours. He wore native dress, married a Malagasy princess, and his son, who went to study in Paris, later became for a while a Malagasy Foreign Minister.[23] With his help and that of other European adventurers, the Malagasy government came to control a small merchant fleet, operated distilleries and sugar plantations, and shared the benefit of an organized monopoly over all the export and import trade with the outside world.

All this was an indication neither of real economic development nor of social progress. It indicated a symbiotic relationship between a small number (not more than a dozen) of European adventurers, and a tyrannical, isolated, xenophobic and traditionalist native government. But it was also a perfect example of what technical advisers could achieve in certain favourable conditions. The fact that the adventurers were 'marginal' men who had, for a variety of reasons, run away from their own societies – French, Greek or American –; the fact that they were often quite uninhibited by their national or religious feelings (Laborde's guns repulsed a Franco–British landing on the shores of Madagascar in 1845, and the most terrible persecution of Christians took place while he was an influential adviser at the Malagasy court); that they acted on a strictly mercenary basis – all this did not alter the fact that as vehicles of change and innovation, and as promoters of modernization, they were superbly successful. In a country without a monetary system or a paid administration, they could mobilize capital for investment. In a society without an educational system, they could create a framework of technical training which provided hundreds of indigenous skilled workers and craftsmen. In a state which lived secluded from the rest of the world, which regarded religious changes and foreign influence as dangerous evils, they could persuade the governing class to spend millions on foreign markets to purchase the tools which would create industrial and agricultural enterprises, some of which present-day Madagascar has not yet been able to achieve. The price, in human labour and suffering, was enormous, but the results were spectacular, and the answer to the question of how they did it can be as relevant to modern planners of technical aid as it has been intriguing to students of Malagasy history.

c. *The Import of the Case*

The fact that these innovators were people who, by choice or of necessity, stood in a certain sense on the margin of their own society and of the society in which they decided to operate, is not in itself an explanation of their ability to act as good or bad vehicles of culture.

The concept of the marginal man as 'an incidental product of a process of acculturation', as observed by Robert E. Park,[24] refers much less to a personality trait than to an expression of a process. The existence of a hybrid, whether social or cultural,[25] does not in itself, however, help us to understand why the same marginal person who appears at one moment (like Jean Laborde in Madagascar) to be a resourceful vehicle of innovation, progress and transculturation, becomes on another occasion an obstacle and a cause of frustration, stagnation, decay – and generally a focus of resistance to transculturation (again, as Jean Laborde turned out to be).[26]

There is little difficulty in accepting the thesis that the marginal man is 'the key personality in the contacts of culture . . . the crucible of cultural fusion', and that the 'practical efforts of the marginal person to solve his own problem lead him consciously or unconsciously to change the situation itself'.[27] Men who are satisfied with themselves and deeply embedded in their own culture do not usually seek to move away, physically or spiritually, from the place in which they have made a nest for themselves. The history of transculturation is also the history of migration – peaceful or otherwise – of men and ideas. But this again does not yet help us to understand why some 'marginal' individuals are good vehicles of culture and others are not.

The link between marginality and effectiveness in the process of transculturation is misleading because it overstresses the psychological and individual aspect of transculturation itself. This aspect is certainly important, and the story of Madagascar's early attempts at modernization is a case in point. But the role of the Europeans in that country in the nineteenth century could equally well be described by calling them 'amphibious' persons, men who had learned to live equally well in two different worlds. Admittedly, their psychological motivations were of some importance; but what was essential was the ability to adapt themselves to different situations well enough and for long enough to be able to translate the ideas or aspirations of one world into the actions of the other, in a manner acceptable to both.

The ability of a carrier of innovation to act in a way acceptable to himself and to others, is very much the ability of a 'man-in-between' to act as a true insider (remember the British missionaries at the beginning of their Madagascar mission, or James Hastie). This is the role which Georg Simmel – we recall – has attributed to the stranger[28] and which, by an extension of his reasoning, could be opposed by the role of the foreigner.

The stranger, to repeat Simmel's phrase, is the man who 'comes today and stays tomorrow'; not the physical wanderer but the 'potential' one;

although he has not moved on, he has not quite overcome the freedom of coming and going. He is fixed within a particular spatial group, or within a group whose boundaries are similar to spatial boundaries. But his position in this group is determined, essentially, by the fact that he has not belonged to it from the beginning, that he imports qualities into it which do not and cannot stem from the group itself.

Is this not a good description of the Madagascar aristocrats who first turned Christian even before they were formally baptized?

The stranger, like the poor and like the sundry 'inner enemies', is an element of the group itself. His position as a full-fledged member involves both being outside it and confronting it. . . . Insofar as members do not leave the circle in order to buy [outside products] – in which case *they* are the 'stranger' merchants in that outside territory – the trader *must* be a stranger, since nobody else has a chance to make a living.

And in this way Simmel captures the role of our European traders in Madagascar.

Thus, the one prototype of the stranger for Simmel is the trader – trader in goods between closed economic societies, trader in ideas – an apt description for the European in pre-colonial Madagascar, which equally fits the more contemporary 'carriers of transculturation', whether they are traders in ideology, technical aid experts, expatriates in the underdeveloped countries, or expatriate students and trainees from underdeveloped countries in more developed ones. Their motivation for filling the role of middleman, or keeper of the gate,[29] may in many cases derive from their psychological marginalism, but this is a secondary aspect of the problem; the major problem faced by the man-in-the-middle, irrespective of whether he is marginal or not, is his relation to authority. What better example for this can I produce than the scene of the first British Agent, accompanied by the first missionary, kneeling before King Radama I at Tananarive.

On this point, too, Simmel has some interesting, though not fully developed thoughts. He notes that the stranger is 'by nature, not an "owner of the soil"; soil not only in the physical but also in the figurative sense of a *life-substance* which is fixed, if not in a point in space, at least in an ideal point of the social environment'. Was it not the military improvement which the British brought to Tananarive that touched the very life substance of the kingdom, namely the slave trade?

Every student of colonial history knows the weight of 'ownership of the soil' in the relations between different societies, especially when one of them is stronger than the other. In pre-colonial Madagascar, one of the permanent sources of trouble between the missionaries and the government was the different conception held by both sides of real estate property, particularly when it was a question of a house which served as a church, or of native slaves serving foreign masters.[30] But ownership is not only material possession; it is also a matter of moral, psychological, cultural, and often metaphysical possession, indeed a 'life substance', to use Simmel's expression – over which men want control as much as they want to keep a material (individual or collective) hold on property. This more impalpable type of possession also derives its rights from traditional legitimacy.

The 'possession of title or status as a result of acquisition by means that are or are held to be according to law or custom' (to quote the definition of legitimacy in Webster's dictionary), is thus often a firmer possession than that of the soil.

There is a yet more subtle aspect of legitimacy, namely the one which – I quote Webster again – indicates a 'conformity to recognized principles'. 'Ownership' of rules and principles is less evident but still very relevant to the process of transculturation and to the stranger who is involved in this process. For Simmel – and also for the Queen of Madagascar – the stranger should not be an 'owner of the soil' in the material and metaphysical sense attributed, in this context, to the word 'soil'. His domain is the domain of 'mobility', since he is not restricted to any 'soil'. His power resides not in ownership but in his objectivity, his ability to adapt himself to the world surrounding him even if he does not belong to it.

As against this stranger, we have seen that there is another wanderer (who Simmel does not take the trouble to define) easily identifiable in contrast to the stranger, namely the foreigner: the man 'who comes today and goes away tomorrow'; the man for whom 'possession of the soil' is of primary concern; the person, or group, who, when acting to achieve possession – in the wider sense described above – does so in accordance with his own type and concept of legitimacy. Force, not persuasion, and partiality, not objectivity, are his prerogatives. He is either in or out of society. The obvious prototype of the foreigner is the military conquerer, but although force is an obvious ingredient of the foreigner's behaviour, it need not necessarily be physical, military might: a man can also be a foreigner through total lack of force, like the slave. The idea mentioned earlier, taken from ancient Mesopotamia (see pp. 54–5), indicates this quite clearly. Between these two extreme types of foreigner, there can always be many degrees of foreignness.

The first British missionaries in Madagascar were obviously foreigners, who, however, acted as strangers: they introduced a lot of innovations, but kept their final aim – religious conversion – for themselves. The British military and political advisers were also foreigners, who for a while came into the stranger category. The drill they introduced into the army was British, but the disciplinary code remained Malagasy;[31] the battle plans were British, as were the organizational solutions to logistic problems, but the decisions remained Malagasy.[32]

As for the adventurers, up to the late 1850s they were prototypes of the stranger described by Schutz and Simmel: in and out of the native society, attracted by the adventurous appeal of and confrontation with the members of the indigenous in-group and fully accepting for a time the legitimacy of its authority (though applying to its interpretation a logic different from that of the natives) and never attempting to impose their own moral principles with suggestions for innovation, but at the same time holding on to a freedom of judgement and of customs which elicited both jealousy and respect among the natives. When the interests of the two groups, the adventurers and the Malagasy, fitted together, so much the better: when they did not, as in the case of openly organizing their own religious life,[33] they found adequate – even if hypocritical – solutions.

These same individuals – missionaries, political and military advisers, adventurers – all turned into foreigners during the latter part of their stay in Madagascar. The missionaries insisted on making their 'technical aid' conditional on the spreading of their religious teaching, which in the meantime had come to be regarded by the traditional élite as the basis of a political movement; the second British Resident attached far more importance to British protocol than to his becoming an accepted insider in the Malagasy upper class, as his predecessor had been; the adventurers put the influence they had acquired as an élite in the Malagasy society at the service of their respective countries, hoping passionately to be recognized there as an élite, despite their long estrangement. The British missionaries and the adventurers, during the first part of their stay in Madagascar, accepted the (military and political) logic of the Malagasy élites, in their choice and promotion of innovations. They received, in exchange, enormous power, which although resented by the masses, was never challenged by them as long as it appeared backed by native traditional authority. As a result, both missionaries and adventurers were able to achieve extraordinary results, in spite of their small numbers, the lack of capital and technical resources, and the distance from sources of western technology.

In the second part of their stay in Madagascar, on the other hand, when for quite different reasons the missionaries and the adventurers ceased to accept native authority as the sole basis of their innovating work, they soon came to be regarded as enemies. Their activities were brought to an abrupt stop: their schools, factories, and farms destroyed; their personal influence reduced to nil, to be only partially restored by foreign colonial conquest.

The key to an understanding of the succession of events in Madagascar in the nineteenth century is not so much the battle between French and British imperialisms in the western Indian Ocean, as the battle between foreign and native legitimization of modernization in the Malagasy society itself. To a considerable extent it remains the key to Malagasy political behaviour during the years of French colonial rule.[34]

2. THE PEACE CORPS CASE

a. *The Historical Setting*
If we wish to find in modern times a technical aid framework which shows some similarities to the modernization efforts of the

European missionaries and adventurers in pre-colonial times we may well look at the experiences of the various – quasi-missionary – peace corps which have been organized by many governments since 1960, and perhaps preferably to the most articulate of them all, the American Peace Corps.[35] A natural outcome of President Kennedy's political philosophy of the New Frontiers, the Peace Corps was in part also to be a reaction against the stereotyped image of the 'Ugly American'. In terms of my present study, one may say, perhaps, that the Peace Corps was intended to constitute the opposite pole of the dichotomy between stranger and foreigner, namely to play the role of the stranger. The ideal qualities of a Peace Corps worker have been suggested[36] as volunteering sensitivity, humility, and cultural proficiency. All these are supposed to counteract the Peace Corps worker's ethnocentricity, and enhance the opposite awareness of cultural relativity. (I do not say this in order to endorse cultural relativism; I simply describe the ideology of the Peace Corps as I read it.) This change of heart had to be achieved through intensive training projects designed to be taken by the volunteers before they were sent into the field (rather than simultaneously).[37] Possibly what was viewed as the most important item in their training was the acquisition of a command of the languages which would enable them to communicate with the people they were going to help. The ability to converse in the local language or dialect is undoubtedly a prime criterion for the conferring of stranger status. A prior knowledge of the local culture was also deemed an important factor, enabling the volunteer in the field to adapt rapidly to local patterns and norms of behaviour. A further basic tenet of Peace Corps ideology was the assumption that the small-scale nature of its projects would make a profound impact at the local level.

The intentions of the Peace Corps theoreticians are all highly laudable, of course, but what I wish to examine is the performance and the practical impact of Peace Corps activities. Fortunately, I found great help in an excellent book, edited by Robert B. Textor: *Cultural Frontiers of the Peace Corps*. In it, a number of anthropologists and sociologists evaluate the initial Peace Corps projects. The book is objective insofar as it indicates both successes and failures of various projects, and thus frees me from much labour. I shall pick from it two cases, representing one success and one failure, in order to provide relevant data for the key concepts of this study – stranger and foreigner, and micro-cooperation.

b. *The Peru Case*

The case of a Peace Corps project in the hacienda Vicos,[38] situated in the Sierra of Peru, is a salutary example of the importance of the relationship between innovator and recipient. The pan-Peruvian attitude towards North Americans is expressed in the rather pejorative term 'gringo', which could aptly be translated as 'foreigner'. The practical application of the term describes the view, conscious or unconscious, of the innovator, held by the local population. The traditional, 'Ugly American' *gringo* had made little progress in Peru, and the question to be asked is whether the Peace Corps were able to change their status *vis-à-vis* the local population.

The population of the Peruvian Sierra consists of two main groups: the urban, Spanish-speaking *mestizos*, and the rural, Quechua-speaking Indians. The relationship between the two groups is basically a classical example of a peasant society with its patron–client relationship (the *mestizos* being the patrons), with a correlated dichotomy of high and low cultures. In the Province of Ancash, where Vicos is situated, the Peace Corps volunteers found themselves gravitating more and more towards the *mestizo* population in their social relationships. This alienated them from the Indian population, whom they were supposed to be assisting, and lost them any claim to the status of 'stranger'. Not only did they not shed the appelation *gringo*, but they now assumed the role of 'patron' themselves, so closely were they associated with the *mestizos* in the minds of the Indians.

All this is reflected in the particular project which the Peace Corps volunteers attempted to carry out in Vicos. The village of Vicos was, in fact, a former manor with a population of about 2,000 souls, dispersed on the manorial land, extending over 30,000 acres. Although the Peace Corps volunteers' experience started in October 1962, the community of Vicos had already been the object of a long and detailed programme of development, initiated in 1952 with a joint project of Cornell University and the Peruvian Ministry of Labour and Indian Affairs.

Adjacent to Vicos was a property called Chaucos which, until

1933, had been an integral part of Vicos. In that year it was rented separately, together with thirteen resident families, whose status was that of serfs. These thirteen families wished to rejoin Vicos, and the people of Vicos were favourably disposed to purchase the Chaucos property. On this property was a decrepit hotel, which had at one time served to accommodate visitors to the local thermal springs. The Peace Corps volunteers regarded this hotel as having an excellent commercial potential for the community, and arranged for its purchase, improvement and refurbishing, through loans from an American bank.

By the time the project reached the construction stage, the relationship between the inhabitants of Vicos and the Peace Corps volunteers was at its lowest ebb. On their side, the Vicosinos did not understand the commercial implications of the project, and even suspected that the American bank loans might in the long run cost them their lands. These doubts caused the project to drag on, whereas the volunteers were naturally anxious to get it going. Instead of recognizing the problem and trying to solve it with and through the local élite, i.e. the local council, the Peace Corps volunteers rushed the project through as if it were in their own interests. During the construction phase they hired and fired workers, gave orders and imposed rigid work schedules, selected people for responsible tasks who were *persona non grata* with the local community, and in fact, made just about every mistake possible in the circumstances. Their status was identical with that of the exploiting *mestizo* patron, and it is no wonder, therefore, that within a relatively short time, the community council demanded the suspension of the project and the expulsion of the Peace Corps volunteers from the area.

Professor Paul L. Doughty, an anthropologist from Indiana University with considerable field experience in aid-to-development work in Latin America, has analysed the problems encountered by the Peace Corps volunteers in Vicos, in an article called 'Pitfalls and Progress in the Peruvian Sierra', from which I have drawn most of the information used in the following pages. To Professor Doughty, the main difficulties encountered by the volunteers were social, cultural and organizational. As we have pointed out above, the Peace Corps volunteers working in the Vicos area found themselves attracted more by the *mestizos*, who were closer to them from the point of view of education and interests, than by the Indians, whose economic and social condition they aimed to ameliorate. What made their social affinity with the *mestizos* easier was the matter of language. Theoretically, the Americans and the indigenous population could understand each other in Spanish. In fact, it was soon realized that, as far as the Indians were concerned, it was the local vernacular – Quechua – which was the best means of communication. This difficulty had not been foreseen in the training programme of the Vicos volunteers. The result was that the only volunteer to be completely successful, and who was not expelled like the others from Vicos, was a teacher who had learned to speak Quechua. 'The inability to make oneself understood properly was at the root of the crisis in Vicos', says Professor Doughty. It is true, of course, that the communication problem can be overcome in part by the use of interpreters, but this technique creates great impersonality.

The Indians also felt that in the particular case of the Peace Corps volunteers they were dealing with foreigners of a degraded status. It was natural for the Indians to compare them with the Americans who had been working in the same village for years under the auspices of the University of Cornell development scheme. The comparison was not favourable to the Peace Corps volunteers. The very fact that they had agreed to live in conditions of relative poverty, though it did not deprive them of the 'racial' status as foreigners who belonged to a powerful alien society, took away some of the prestige they should have possessed by virtue of being 'rich Americans'. In this sense they automatically earned less respect than the Cornell group.

Both the volunteers and the Cornell group were sincerely involved in their work, but the veteran Cornell group had acquired, through protracted residence and close working relations with the indigenous population, a more detached and realistic view of what could be done and how. The volunteers had greater expectations which led to considerable frustration. For this reason they acted in a more hectic way, and this in turn diminished their authority. Finally, the two groups, as so often happens with small expatriate communities, developed strong feelings of antagonism among themselves, which reduced even further the respect in which they were held by the native population.

The Peace Corps volunteers undoubtedly had a deep sense of mission. Unfortunately, to be well-intentioned and devoted to one's task does not necessarily imply that one is sure of oneself and of one's ideas. In fact, all the personnel involved in post-war aid-to-development schemes are far more sensitive to feelings of hostility among native populations than were the administrators of the old colonies, or the missionaries in pre-colonial times. This is not necessarily due to the pattern of relations with the local population. It is the outcome of a long, soul-searching process which has been going on within the European mind and culture during the last two generations, and which has raised many doubts concerning the essence and values of western culture itself. Whether the Peace Corps volunteers consciously put this question to themselves or not, the fact remains that during the 1960s no white man, either at home or abroad, was able to share the feelings of racial, religious, political and cultural superiority of the white man a hundred years earlier. If one is not convinced of the superior quality of the goods one is offering, how can one be totally persuasive while selling them, especially when face to face with the potential buyer? The sense of the justness of one's cause with which the nineteenth-century missionaries were so deeply imbued was lacking among the Peace Corps volunteers, and this accounted for much of their reduced status and authority in the eyes of the natives. Social uncertainty was the result of moral and cultural uncertainty.

Another important obstacle, also inherent in the Americans, was their impatience, the desire of most volunteers to 'do something', to see quick results, to fulfil the high expectations with which they had come to their new area of activity. This gave them a sense of urgency which was heightened by the many frustrating delays caused by having to deal with unconcerned bureaucracy, linguistic barriers and personality conflicts. In the case of Vicos, impatience was also increased by the different tempo of working habits of the Cornell group and the Peace Corps, the latter operating according to a logic and method of development of their own.

This type of situation, though in very different circumstances, recalls some of the problems which faced the European carriers of innovation in nineteenth-century Madagascar. There, too, the foreign importers of change had to face linguistic problems, and to become accustomed to working within the traditional, local culture, if they wanted to achieve results. There, too, there was status friction inside and outside the expatriate groups. One cannot, admittedly, find in old Madagascar a contingent of *mestizos*, but one of the causes of conflict between the British missionaries and the Malagasy tradition was the fact that the cultural affinities between the missionaries and the people trained in their schools or converted to their religion were closely linked with political and economic vested interests. What was certainly different in the two situations, as we pointed out earlier, was that the Europeans in pre-colonial Madagascar possessed, and the Peace Corps volunteers lacked, a deep-rooted sense of superiority. In the former case, the carriers of innovation had no doubts about the superiority of their religion or the justice of their civilizing cause. They could be completely magnanimous because they were completely sure of the ultimate success of their mission, if not of their own personal mission. In the case of the Peace Corps volunteers the opposite was usually the case. They had, it is true, joined the Corps out of a sense of devotion and sacrifice towards the people of the less developed countries, but they were not certain, and had clearly not been trained to believe, that they belonged to a superior civilization. And to be superior in means but not in values does not contribute to one's intellectual security. Be that as it may, what seems clear is that despite the differences and the time gap, what brought the Peace Corps experience in Vicos to an end was more or less the same constellation of factors that ended the missionary experience in Madagascar many years earlier. It can be summed up as the inability to obtain legitimization of innovation by the local traditional authority.

In the case of Vicos, it was the attempts of the volunteers to push through an entrepreneurial scheme, logical and economically sound, but totally unassimilable by the indigenous leadership, which eventually led to an open break between the volunteers and the local population, and the ultimate expulsion of the former.

Doughty suggests that in the Vicos case the Peace Corps group overlooked one of the basic assumptions of organizational work, namely that successful community development projects must have the general support and interest of the people in order to succeed. This is the point at which I disagree with his conclusions.

The need for a project, he claims, must be felt by a majority of the community and not just by the development workers. But, if the claim of micro-cooperation is correct, the key to success in a development project is not really the agreement of the majority of the community, but agreement between the development workers and the legitimizing élite. Obviously the volunteers made a lot of mistakes in Vicos: the most blatant was their attempt to substitute themselves, consciously or unconsciously, for an indigenous élite. This made them total foreigners and created fundamental misunderstandings, even about the best-intentioned activities. For instance, the money obtained as a loan by the community for development purposes and handled directly by the volunteers created suspicions that the *gringos* were misappropriating the funds.

However, even if the volunteers had not made such obvious mistakes, they would probably still not have been successful in their work, because they did not try, first to identify, and then to cooperate with the élite which should have promoted and diffused the innovation. They were asking people to engage in activities according to their own foreign standards and abilities, instead of helping them to adopt the innovation and adapt and use it according to their own understanding. The fact that the volunteers enjoyed a smaller or larger consensus for their activities had little to do with the aim of the activities themselves, namely to help people to help themselves, and not just to help them without even asking if they wanted to be helped.

c. *The Afghanistan Case*

The dichotomy between the role of the foreigner and that of the stranger is underlined again in an entirely different example of micro-cooperation, carried out by Peace Corps volunteers in Afghanistan. It has been described by Louis Dupree, an anthropologist from Harvard who has seen a lot of field work in Afghanistan, in a paper entitled 'Moving Mountains in Afghanistan' from which I have drawn the information for the following account.

The idea of sending Peace Corps volunteers to Afghanistan came from the American Director of the Afghan Institute of Technology, Mr Cleo Shook. He persuaded the Afghan Government of the 'purity of the Peace Corps' and induced them to accept an initial group of volunteers, despite strong anti-American, Soviet propaganda, the Afghan fear of jeopardizing their neutrality between the two super-powers, and the concern of the local government that the Soviets might, in their turn, offer to flood the country with young Soviet pioneers to counteract the Americans.

In this case, also, we find many similarities with the Malagasy experience, and first of all the 'diplomatic breakthrough' to the suspicious local government, due to the trust of the Afghan authorities in the personal integrity of one man. In the case of Afghanistan it was Cleo Shook; in the case of nineteenth-century Madagascar it was James Hastie. Like Madagascar in the nineteenth century, Afghanistan looked like the worst possible country for a Peace Corps operation. Afghanistan has for centuries been a Moslem country, isolated from the rest of the world by its extreme geographical harshness. Dupree describes it like this:

Until the late 1950s, practically no roads worthy of the name existed, and Kabul, the capital, had no adequately paved streets. Almost no wheeled vehicles could be found in Afghan villages, and donkeys, camels, horses, mules and even cattle served for transport. A notoriously incompetent telecommunications system made overall government supervision and control difficult or impossible, except in zones of easy accessibility.

An oligarchy of the Royal Family ruled, and the government, although oriented towards development in the economic sense, suppressed political opposition. A continuing border problem with Pakistan effectively closed Afghanistan's economic relations with the West several times between 1947 and 1963. There is little socioeconomic mobility. Civil servants remain underpaid, and – in order to survive – continue to accept 'baksheesh' for anticipated services. Clerks, often the product of nepotism, clutter up offices, laboriously recording data which the government seldom uses.

Given these facts, it is no wonder that superficial observers see Afghanistan as being a backward, conservative, landlocked, relatively isolated, lethargic, illiterate, priest-ridden country with little past and less future.

In this close-knit and inward-looking society, strengthened by tribal custom and local Islamic tradition, everything seemed to work against the idea of developing innovation through the import of foreign carriers of change. The first Peace Corps volun-

teers in Afghanistan, like the first British missionaries in Madagascar, were not only regarded as suspect aliens, but also as people
of undefined social status, halfway between the powerful western
foreigner (personified by the diplomat) and the weak indigenous
middle class. They belonged to a different culture, prayed to a
different God, and when they did not pray at all they were regarded as atheists which was even worse. Their culture was different, their tastes strange, their reactions unpredictable, their true
motives unknown. They had to be closely watched, if for no other
reason than because in Afghanistan, as in most non-western underdeveloped countries, 'a man is born into a set of answers, while in
an outward looking western society, a man is born into a set of
questions'. The Afghans did not want the Peace Corps volunteers to
put too many questions, to which they knew they had no answers.
It was the great merit of the first group of Peace Corps volunteers
not to try to substitute their own answers for those of the indigenous élite. Nor did they antagonize the conservative leadership.
They elected to set a standard and an example, patiently waiting
for their standards and examples to be picked up by the indigenous
population. They introduced change into the traditional milieu
without appearing to interfere, or, at least, trying to interfere as
little as possible.

The first nine volunteers to arrive in Afghanistan (6 women – 3
English teachers and 3 nurses, and 3 men – 2 English teachers and
1 mechanic) quickly realized that, contrary to their initial wish
and plan, they would have to work in Kabul, the capital city,
rather than in the outlying districts. This was the first correct decision, because by staying near the centre of traditional authority
they could be more easily observed by the government authorities,
without whose agreement no innovating activity could be carried
out. For several months they worked without receiving any hint as
to whether their activities were appreciated or not. But when, in
the spring of 1963, the Peace Corps Representative in Kabul asked
the Afghan Government whether it wanted some additional volunteers, he was surprised by a request to multiply their number by
ten, and to send the new people to work outside Kabul.

One year later the Peace Corps had become an institution and a
going concern in Afghanistan, and the Government asked the
Peace Corps authorities to increase the number of volunteers to

several hundred. 'Simply by working with Afghans at the middle and lower levels, the Peace Corps volunteers made an impact, though it is often invisible, and this naturally disturbs the volunteers,' writes Dupree.

Peace Corps activities in Afghanistan were undoubtedly highly successful as far as the image of the American technical adviser was concerned. The fact that the Afghan Government requested more and more volunteers left no doubt about this point. But the only conclusion that one can draw from this request is that the volunteers projected a very favourable image of themselves and of their government. This does not necessarily imply that they were also successful in their task of promoting aid-to-development, and in fact they did not succeed in creating a multiplying and self-reproducing effect in their work. Insofar as their activities were appreciated, they were not asked – as were the missionaries in pre-colonial Madagascar – to train indigenous teachers who could, in turn, train more indigenous pupils. They were simply asked to come to Afghanistan in ever increasing numbers, to take over more or less limited but always direct responsibilities, and to supply cheap, trained manpower.

The evidence brought by Dupree is insufficient to permit a final judgement to be made on the matter. One must, however, note that in the case of a skilled and energetic volunteer, who moved into an automotive workshop and succeeded in improving its level of operations, his personal success did not mean a successful transfer of knowledge. The mechanic, thanks to his personality, his face-to-face contact with the Afghan personnel, and his ability to improvise with local materials, had worked miracles. When his assignment came to an end in June 1969, and his Afghan superiors did not request a replacement for him, several of the changes he had instituted quickly faded away. 'His case,' comments Dupree, 'again demonstrates the necessity for suspended outside impetus in order to catalyse, achieve and *perpetuate* change at the workday level. It also demonstrates the simple fact that such a change cannot be perpetuated unless reasonably strong cooperation is received from key local officials.' This is the central point in the whole argument about aid-to-development, and is probably the only yardstick by which such aid itself should be judged.

d. *Conclusions to be Drawn from Peace Corps Activities*

While the aims of the Peace Corps obviously constitute an honest attempt to establish a new dimension in development aid, the performance and impact of the programmes themselves remain questionable. Dupree sums up the substantial differences between traditional American assistance programmes and the Peace Corps programme in Afghanistan as follows:

In the past, American assistance programs usually consisted of money (grants and loans) and technical assistance – without any guarantees of continuity. Under such conditions, the result can be a dam, a road, or a university left empty and functionless on the landscape of a developing country – a magnificent ruin. Tractors and buses with no provisions for spare parts or maintenance often sit idle and useless for months.[39]

This coincides with the general contention of this study, that change in environment alone is not a significant contribution to development. Dupree continues in the same vein:

The Peace Corps volunteers, especially in Afghanistan, try to fill these longitudinal needs, to continue the processes begun. They try to do this gently, within the cultural pattern, and not with a heavy, alien, self-righteous hand. This patient, day-to-day, face-to-face contact continuity. Under such conditions, the result can be a dam, a road, or to introduce and *perpetuate* the ideas which stimulate technological change. . . .[40]

I am particularly happy to have quoted the above sentence. The operative phrase here is 'to introduce and *perpetuate* the ideas which stimulate permanent technological change'. There is no evidence from Dupree's description of the Afghanistan case that this aim was, in fact, achieved. Dupree's criterion of success is the progressive institutionalization of the Peace Corps in Afghanistan, rather than the performance of any given programme. It would be a truism to say that the changing of ideas is a long process: ideas do change in time, but what we are discussing here is an induced process of change, to be effected within a relatively short period of time.

Good intentions, the attempt to reduce ethnocentricity and the consequent recognition of cultural relativity, are all steps in the right direction. Let us even assume that the Peace Corps volunteers in Afghanistan were trying to achieve the status of stranger as opposed to foreigner. It is still quite clear that they were not using this status in any kind of strategy to activate the local population on a significant scale. The Peace Corps groups came and went, fulfilling their limited functions by carrying out their respective jobs. By some inexplicable process of osmosis, it is assumed that they had imbued the existing system with their new ideas. This can hardly be regarded as a serious attempt to effect change.

The Peruvian example illustrates the extreme difficulty involved in the process of acquiring the status of stranger. The contrast between the Peruvian and the Afghanistan examples is particularly instructive. While in Afghanistan the practical aims of the project remain patently unclear, the limited aim of the Peruvian project, i.e. the purchase and operation of a hotel, was clearly stated. When faced with a specific technological innovation (in this case the introduction of a commercial enterprise), the Peace Corps volunteers behaved no differently from traditional American carriers of innovation. They acted like true, stereotypical foreigners. By setting themselves apart from the Indian community and reinforcing their foreigner status by association with the *mestizos*, they nullified all their efforts to change the ideas of the Indian community. The project became merely a pragmatic consideration of operating a hotel, which the volunteers were prepared to push through, even at the expense of their own status. Operating a hotel in Vicos differs only in scale from erecting a huge dam or an industrial complex. Even if the Peace Corps had succeeded in establishing this venture, it is doubtful whether it would have had any significant effect.

The most obvious lesson to be learned from Peace Corps experience is the one I wish to illustrate, namely, that the difficulty of reconciling a given aim with a given strategy is best overcome the easy way. Where the Peace Corps volunteers in Peru failed was, firstly, in not recognizing the importance of imparting commercial know-how to the Indians of Vicos, so that the hotel enterprise might change their way of thinking, and secondly – and more important – in their inability to act as strangers and thus influence the local élite, i.e. the local community council, to activate the project themselves. This same inability to reconcile a project with a strategy is apparent also in the Afghanistan case, where the volunteers tried to achieve stranger status in order to influence their Afghan counterparts, but without having any clear direction in mind.

The Role of the Social Catalyst

To draw a direct comparison between a case of modernization carried out by missionaries and adventurers in a pre-colonial country like nineteenth-century Madagascar, and cases of modernization carried out by the American Peace Corps in the second half of the twentieth century, would obviously be a useless exercise.

And yet, in both cases, the human element – represented by the carrier of innovation – remains an essential link in the process of modernization. W. B. Heath, an anthropologist closely connected with Peace Corps activities in Bolivia,[41] has stressed the importance of the Peace Corps volunteers and their 'sub-culture', namely the 'distinctive set of understandings, of values, and even of jargon'[42] which is peculiar to more or less all groups of Peace Corps volunteers. In the case of Bolivia, which he has studied, Heath points out eight main elements or patterns making up the Peace Corps sub-culture. These are: an energetic activity; egoistic altruism; proud humility; local identification; realistic idealism; planned expediency; situational austerity; and organizational loyalty.[43] All these patterns, which are certainly correct, point to the very egocentric outlook of the members of the most altruistic technical aid organization which has ever been established for the purpose of contributing to development. Furthermore, many of these patterns are the same as those shown by the missionaries and adventurers of old. We could certainly find clear-cut cases of energetic activity, egoistic altruism, proud humility, local identification (to the point of becoming local patriots), austerity, and a lot of planned expediency, in the Malagasy case. But what distinguishes the activities of the missionaries and adventurers from those of the Peace Corps volunteers, and what probably explains the extraordinary success of the former and the small impact of the latter, is the different concept and position held by the two groups towards the indigenous recipient society, as *a legitimizing élite*. The missionaries and the adventurers, whatever their personal abilities, motivations and inclinations, regarded the Malagasy ruling class as being superior to themselves in status. They realized that if they wanted to promote their innovations they had to have them approved, accepted and diffused by the indigenous *élite*, and that therefore they had to adapt their own values and concepts to those of the local rulers, insofar as they were also the legitimizing authority for the diffusion of any specific innovation.

In the case of the Peace Corps this was never the case. Because the indigenous élite was always aware of the social, technological, political, and in many cases also cultural, superiority of the American society, right from the outset the status relationship could not be that of a stranger/innovator looking up to a local élite, or that of an indigenous élite looking down upon a stranger/innovator. On the contrary, it was always a relationship between foreigners, which persisted even when on-the-spot personal contacts were characterized (on the part of the volunteers) by friendship, humility, altruism and a high degree of idealism. It is interesting that even when the Peace Corps volunteers 'got off their pedestal',[44] they could not be treated by the local élite as equals or inferiors (a situation which might have favoured the acceptance of the innovation) because, consciously or unconsciously, the volunteers were perceived as members of a superior and foreign, colonial or semi-colonial élite, which has been for generations the sole expression of the western presence in underdeveloped countries.

It is this difficulty in breaking away from an image of foreignness that has limited so greatly the impact of the Peace Corps. Where they succeeded for their personal qualities – and in many cases they succeeded beyond imagination – they created a great demand for replacement after their completion of duty. But this is the very crux of the matter: replacement of good foreigners was requested *instead* of the local élite and local personnel taking over from the volunteers. This problem is clearly envisaged by Robert B. Textor in the final chapter of his book, when he discusses the conclusions, the problems and the prospects connected with and facing the Peace Corps. There is no doubt that he is correct when he states that the volunteers have contributed immensely to improving the American image overseas, and that they have achieved within the American society a cultural sensitivity and proficiency which was previously lacking. However, when it comes to the contribution to the development of the host countries, continues Textor, it appears that while the volunteers provided and are providing very important services, they are not usually 'developmentally significant'. 'Making a lasting contribution to the host country's development is by far the most difficult of three objectives outlined or suggested in the Peace Corps Act [meeting the need for trained manpower; promoting a better understanding of the American people by the host country, and promoting a better understanding of other peoples by the American people] [45] principally because it involves many social, cultural, political and administrative factors far beyond the control of the individual volunteer.' [46] Textor also notes that very often innovative contributions are made quite unintentionally, and that the better community developer is the one who resists the temptation of making direct contributions. [47] It is only when the Peace Corps volunteers adopt 'the role of the "social catalyst" and work patiently with the local leaders until they in turn can convince their people that it is time for them to build their "sanitary well" with their own labour and perhaps material', that permanent results are achieved. This is exactly the point which micro-cooperation is meant to underline; and the reason why it is so often missed, in spite of the best intentions of Peace Corps volunteers, is that there is no rationally planned framework through which they could put it into effect. Textor makes this quite plain.

Can a framework be conceived and put into operation so that it achieves 'social catalysis'? Obviously only in cases where efforts of aid-to-development are comprehensive enough to catalyse. How comprehensive? The answer is, I think, where techniques of micro-cooperation are applied within an overall, planned scheme of aid-to-development. The case of development of Arab agriculture on the West Bank of the Jordan by the Israelis, after the war of June 1967, is, in my view, another case in point, and will be discussed in the next chapter. I have chosen to discuss this case because as an Israeli I am familiar with it, and also, incidentally, because it is the only successful, comprehensive case I know. In addition, it is exciting because it is even more astonishing than the Marshall Plan and the lack of hostility shown by the US towards its Second World War foes.

Chapter 5

The Israeli Experience

The cases cited above illustrate the relationship between extraneous carriers of innovation and indigenous authority structures, within the framework of small-scale innovations. The present chapter will discuss the same relationship, but in the context of a comprehensive development scheme in a totally hostile environment. The following specific case study refers to the Israeli development of Arab agriculture on the West Bank of the Jordan after the War of June 1967 and up to the end of 1970.*

*There are few studies dealing with the Israeli administration of Arab territories occupied since the war of June 1967 and those that there are derive mainly from official sources and are by no means comprehensive. Among those published by independent academic sources, Y. Mundlak and G. Avni, *The Effect of Free Trade with the Administered Territories on Israel's Agriculture* (in Hebrew), The Centre for Agricultural Economic Research, Jerusalem, is one of the best. S. Tevet has attempted a comprehensive and vivid interpretation of the Israeli occupation in *The Cursed Blessing*, and G. Weigert a factual presentation in *Arabs and Israelis: Life Together*.

The material for this chapter comes mainly from personal contact with the men on the spot and from the material kindly put at my disposal by Mr Eitan Israely, Assistant Director-General of the Israeli Ministry of Agriculture and former Director of Agriculture on the West Bank. I have tried to describe the techniques employed by him to promote the modernization of West Bank agriculture without touching on the obvious political implications because I feel that, whatever the political motives behind them, they represent an outstanding example of technical cooperation. By 1973 these techniques

A consequence of military conquest can be the imposition of a colonial type régime. Although it has been claimed in certain quarters that this situation followed the Israeli victory in 1967, the point becomes patently irrelevant to the subject matter of this book. What is of importance is that the Israelis intentionally behaved as strangers *vis-à-vis* the Arab population, rather than as foreigners. This resulted in a series of remarkable developments in the traditional agricultural system of the West Bank. The case is brought to support the contention that micro-cooperation serves to promote development. It achieves this by means of the strangers' activation of an élite which legitimizes acceptance of innovation regardless of the political situation.

The Israeli micro-cooperative approach to development was not an *ad hoc* response to the situation created by the post-1967 occupation. The idea has been developed during several decades of building a Jewish State and through the efforts of Israel's technical assistance programmes to other developing countries.

Pragmatism and immigrants

Three main factors have enabled Israel to extend aid to other underdeveloped countries: *pragmatism*, an *immigrant population*, and Israel's *geopolitical situation*.

In Israel, pragmatic attitudes have grown into a strong body of beliefs; so strong, in fact, that a passion for action at times looks like a dangerous substitute for a willingness to think. On the whole, however, it has produced a remarkable flexibility in the interpretation of social and political ideologies, in the translation of these ideologies by the institutions, and a strong appreciation of the 'art' of adaptation of both ideologies and institutions to necessity. A whole lexicon has evolved in Israel to define such an attitude, and, in fact, a whole philosophy of life has matured which makes the 'adaptation approach' a naturally accepted attitude in

---

were fully vindicated by the material results achieved. Their practicability seems now to be receiving additional recognition from certain African countries which – though condemning Israel for its occupation of the West Bank – have shown keen interest in the experience gained and its possible relevance to the modernization of their own agriculture (*Davar*, March 1973).

all training syllabuses. In a country of immigration, adaptation means more than simple compromise. It very often means searching deeply into other people's cultures in order to find bases for establishing common denominators. This, of course, is only one aspect of the type of problem and solution which Israel, as a country of immigrant population, has had to face. Others were linked with the need to find methods of facilitating the integration of the immigrants and blending them into one nation.

Madrichim and Moshavim

One of the important outcomes of this permanent tug-of-war between ideas and realities was the development of a special type of expert – the *Madrich* (guide). The *Madrich* had to be teacher, protector, leader, confidant. He had to develop a thorough knowledge of technical know-how, deep psychological insight, and a quick understanding of a continuously changing situation. He not only represented 'the stable authoritative link between the newcomer and his strange new surroundings, but he also [became] the principal interpreter of the new environment, the channel through which the environment influences and changes the attitude of the newcomer'.[1] Over the years, Israel has produced a vast number of such people. To them has been entrusted the task of teaching the trainees in development sent to Israel by the countries of the Third World.

One of the fields of Israeli society in which social pragmatism and immigration have met in a highly successful union, has been that of cooperative agriculture. Cooperative agricultural communities – the *Moshav* and the *Moshav Shitufi*[2] – helped the immigrants to take root and exchange the traditional skills and trades brought from their own colonial societies for the modern activities of a rapidly changing and westernized state.

In development areas like B'sor and Lachish,[3] the fitting of the cooperative village system into a balanced frame of pre-planned services and regional industries proved extremely successful, not only in meeting local needs, but also in developing techniques of comprehensive planning, in which as much attention was devoted to the psychological and educational problems of a community as to its economic and technical requirements.

It was in these development areas that the new generation of

Madrichim discovered the fallacies inherent in a single-solution, technical approach to development. Many of them later on saw this approach proving a complete failure in the bilateral or multi-lateral aid programmes initiated by the big powers in the under-developed countries of Asia, Africa and Latin America.[4] Again, it was in these *Moshav*-based, comprehensive, regional development programmes that the Israelis learned for themselves that no 'technological package approach' (as opposed to the 'single solution' approach) could become operational without an appropriate insti-tutional package; that price incentives cannot change the trends of traditional production unless accompanied by appropriate pro-vision of services; and, last but not least, that the promotion of comprehensive development calls for more ability in the handling of man than in the manipulation of capital and instruments.[5] Such a handling is never a manipulation of isolated individuals taken out of their milieu: it is a manipulation of men in the setting of their social milieu – which, of course, makes a radical difference. The *Moshav* thus became the blueprint for comprehensive agricultural development.

The *Moshav* served to promote abroad more than just the idea of applied cooperation. To many people it seemed to be a com-prehensive 'tool' of social, economic, cultural and technical progress, which had something to offer to all three models of underdevelopment defined in Galbraith's classification[6] – the sub-Saharan African model, the Latin-American model, and the South Asian model.

The Moshav as a model for agricultural development
The *Moshav* could serve the first of the three as a demonstration prototype of an agricultural village system. With its comprehensive combination of advanced techniques, integrated social and cultural services, and participation by the villagers in the responsibilities of running all stages of local planning implementation, it was capable of providing an answer to the principal barrier to development in Model 1 countries, namely the absence of a minimal cultural base, especially within the élite, which was supposed to take upon itself the task of cooperative administration. The Israeli experience of comprehensively planned development areas proved that the *Moshav* system could produce such an élite even among new

immigrants lacking any agricultural experience and with no technical culture or common cultural ties. This, in fact, was the situation which the Israelis later found in the Central African Republic, Senegal, Dahomey, West and East Nigeria, and elsewhere.

The *Moshav* could offer Galbraith's second model two things: (a) an alternative policy of development, based on micro-techniques, for those governments which had tried out macro-techniques of development (usually in the form of politically inspired land reform) and got stuck for lack of the appropriate planning, personnel or implementation; (b) the possibility of integrating into macro-development plans, which had little appeal for the individual farmer, micro-development schemes which could fire and sustain the enthusiasm of the individuals for local development, while the wider infra-structure of the national plans were being created.

The *Moshav* system obviously had nothing to offer to revolutionaries. Its declared ambition was not to change man or society, but to allow those individuals who wished to improve their economic and social status, to do so within any given society. It stressed the principles and values of social pragmatism far more than those of historical or ideological determinism. It had, however, two valuable solutions to offer to a government which wanted to engage in social evolution. First, it suggested concrete and tested solutions for the practical implementation of agricultural reform, which in many countries lagged behind, not because the authorities were short of good intentions, but because the country lacked trained personnel and appropriate techniques to carry out the reforms. Second, the *Moshav*, as a result of its long ideological competition with the *Kibbutz* and other radical socialist movements in Israel, had acquired sufficient experience and self-confidence to support its own socialist theory of micro-development against the theories of macro-development of Marxist revolutionaries. Its techniques were, in fact, based on the assumption that the faith and enthusiasm of farmers, or other implementers of development plans, could be fired strongly enough and sustained long enough to promote self-sustaining local dynamism and civic pride, if these individuals could be offered quick material incentives combined with understandable ideological rationalization of their planned micro-activities in development. This theory has proved successful in a number of development projects initiated by Israel in Latin America, with local governments' schemes of agrarian reform, as in the case of the El-Sisal Development Project in the Azva Province of the Dominican Republic,[7] or the Puno Scheme in Peru.[8] The theory was so successful, in fact, that Israel is now applying it to other areas of development in Asia and Africa, where the *Moshav* technique was introduced only as a demonstration prototype of an agricultural village system for those areas included in Galbraith's number 1 model of underdevelopment – for instance, in Laos,[9] Nepal[10] and Zambia.[11]

As for Model 3 countries, such as India or Pakistan, where – according to Galbraith's classification of underdevelopment – progress is hampered by a disproportion among the various branches of production, the *Moshav* system has far less relevance because of the difficult land/population ratio coupled with the small size of holdings. Some attempts have, in fact, been made to apply the *Moshav* model to development programmes even in this type of country, but whether because Galbraith's Model 3 countries also happen to be those with whom Israel has either very cool (e.g. India) or no diplomatic relations (e.g. Pakistan and Indonesia), or because their development problems are of an immensity which a small country like Israel cannot tackle, the *Moshav* techniques have so far failed to produce any substantial impact.

Israel's geopolitical situation

Turning now to the geopolitical factor, its importance is illustrated by the Israel development experts' motto that 'Africa (or Latin America, or Asia) begins at home'. This is the underlying belief of the Israeli technical aid programme. The corollary, therefore, is not how to make foreign realities fit the Israeli geographical situation, but how to adapt Israeli techniques to foreign realities.

Some of Israel's geographical features are well adapted to reducing the hiatus between home and abroad. Like many of the underdeveloped countries, Israel enjoys (or suffers from) natural shortcomings: a hot climate, a tendency to soil erosion, drought, and an unequal distribution of rain throughout the year. At the same time it has agricultural diversity, some forms belonging to cold climates and others to tropical ones. Politically speaking, it possesses a basic knowledge of colonial (British) bureaucratic structures, combined with some knowledge of French (North African) colonial systems, and a personal knowledge of colonial rule, with the colonial and anti-colonial 'lingo'. From the social point of view it sports a mosaic of immigrant groups which, to a certain extent, is comparable to the tribal mosaics of Africa, and the coexistence of traditional social structures (the patriarchal family of the Asian and African immigrants, the traditional Arab village) with more modern forms, and of various stages of agricultural development with various stages of industrial ones.

The social structure of Israel is also congenial to the transfer of know-how to foreign trainees. When a Cabinet Minister is seen washing dishes in a *kibbutz*; when farmers belong to the 'upper class' of a country; when dress and housing are not status symbols – it is obviously much easier for a teacher to persuade his pupils to work with their own hands than it would be in a society where manual work is synonymous with social inferiority. Small wonder, therefore, that foreign trainees in Israel should assimilate the teaching imparted to them more quickly and more easily than elsewhere.

Another factor also contributed to the establishment of Israel's pedagogical abilities. Because cooperation budgets were limited; because more instructors speaking the language of trainees (French, English, Spanish or Portuguese) were available at non-academic than at university level; because it proved possible to adapt teaching to students' requirements only within a framework of short courses and not through long-term curricula – for all these reasons Israel specialized in what was known as the technical formation of 'Development NCOs' rather than Officers. This, in turn, made Israeli programmes particularly attractive to foreign governments plagued by the problem of unemployed intellectuals and by the need to form low rank cadres. It also gave Israel an opportunity to acquire great experience in the methodology of technical aid teaching. It is this experience that helped to formulate a sophisticated model for development, to be applied in the administered areas of the West Bank of the Jordan.

Examples of Israel's technical assistance programmes are given in the appendix. We now turn to our main example – the occupied West Bank territories.

Initial indeterminacy

When the Israeli army occupied the West Bank of the Jordan, very few people knew what occupation meant. Certainly no one expected that Israel would be called upon to control a thickly inhabited Arab territory for more than a few months. The only plans which were made were of a purely legal nature: the Army's legal department laid down some basic rules for the occupation authority to act upon, on the basis of the Geneva Convention. One of these basic principles was that the local Military Governor who, in some cases was also a senior officer of fighting units in the area, should also be the man responsible for the continuation of normal civil life. The immediate and important result of this decision – which the divided opinions within the Israeli Government about the future of occupation made more relevant – was that the Army was given, especially at the beginning of the occupation, the upper hand in the administration. This gave to the Defence Ministry – in spite of the government decision that each Ministry should be responsible for its own functional tasks – a decisive voice in the formulation and application of any policy towards the occupied part of Jordan.

Such a policy soon became identified with one person – Mr Moshe Dayan – who, as Minister of Defence, had the *ex officio* responsibility for the occupied territory, but had also, as former Chief of Staff of the Israeli Army during the 1956 Sinai Campaign, dealt with the problems of the occupation of Gaza for about four months.

The experience of the 1956 occupation had been far from positive, both for Israel and for the local inhabitants. The troops entered the Gaza Strip without any idea of what the future of the region would be. They set to work with passion and determination to show the Arab refugees the difference between Egyptian and Israeli military occupation. They received a relatively favourable response from the leaders and the rank and file of the population, which was dearly paid for when the evacuation came. The UNEF (United Nations Emergency Force) administration, which the Israelis accepted as their replacement when they evacuated the Gaza Strip (and which should have protected the Arabs who had collaborated with Israel) was superseded by the Egyptian Military

Administration in less than a week. An unknown number, some say 2,000, some say less, of Arabs (among them the Mayor of Gaza, who was killed) were imprisoned and bullied for their 'treason'. Neither Dayan nor the Arab notables wanted to see such a situation repeated on the West Bank.

During a visit to Vietnam as a press correspondent, Dayan had had many occasions to see (and criticize) the bad effects of excessive American interference in local affairs. The underlying principle of his policy of occupation was therefore 'to leave the Arabs to themselves' as much as possible, and make them solely responsible for a wide range of civil affairs. Apart from the initial indeterminacy, there were other reasons favouring a policy of noninterference. During the summer of 1967, the Israelis were convinced that the occupation would last only a few weeks, possibly a few months, and that peace was very near. Why should Israel teach the Jordanian farmers to improve their agricultural methods, to switch from a line of production not competitive with that of Israeli farmers, to crops which would inevitably compete with their own, and on a basis of cheaper labour? [12]

The Arabs, for their part, had little appreciation of this internal Israeli argument. For them to switch from remunerative export crops for Arab countries to possibly equally remunerative export crops for non-Arab countries via Israel, was – to say the least – highly irritating. It meant accepting the idea of a lengthy occupation of their territories by Israel; it meant losing their direct economic links with Arab markets for less direct and Israeli-controlled contacts with non-Arab, unknown markets in the western world; it meant – above all – embarking on a far-reaching basic transformation of local agriculture in order to produce sufficient quantities of the same quality as that of Jewish farms, to obtain the same prices. Psychologically speaking they were opposed to it, financially and technically they had not the faintest idea of how to set about it, and socially they were dead against it. It meant a change in the traditional relations between landowners and agricultural workers, between farmers and agricultural experts, between farmers and merchants. Each group had its own interest, habits and clear-cut position in society which, if changed, would endanger not only their established economic position but – and this was for more important – personal, family, and often political status.

Problems and improvisations

These problems were further reinforced by two circumstances which the military had little power to change. The first was the Army's lack of manpower. Being a very small, regular army, swelled by the mobilization of well-trained reserves, it could get as many men as were available in the country for fighting, but not for any extra-military duties. The Army, therefore, simply did not have the people to run the occupied territories. Only with great difficulty could it provide the men to defend them from the Arab armies on the outside and the Palestine guerrillas on the inside.

The second circumstance, which lent support to Dayan's policy of non-intervention in civil affairs, was the fact that the West Bank had not been run by the Jordanians as a geographical or economic unit. The area, consisting of some 6,000 square kilometres with about 700,000 inhabitants (some had left; a third were refugees from the 1948 Arab-Israeli war) was run, for reasons of political and bureaucratic convenience, directly from Amman, as three separate units: Nablus in the north – capital of Samaria; Hebron in the south – capital of Southern Judea, and Jerusalem in the centre. These three districts (after the annexation of Jerusalem, Ramallah became the seat of the former Jerusalem District) had no experience of autonomous administration at even the lowest administrative echelons. The Mayors were chosen by the Government in Amman; all departments – agriculture, health, posts and education – were directly dependent on Amman.

Furthermore, the three districts had different social and economic structures as well as different political traditions. Samaria was thickly populated whereas Southern Judea was not. Samaria's population was engaged in agriculture, based on yearly crops, on fairly flat ground or valleys; Hebron's mountain population included a large proportion of Bedouin, and cultivated permanent plantations on hilly ground. Furthermore, Hebron was the centre of political loyalty to the Hashemite crown and was solidly traditional. Samaria and the Nablus District had been the traditional cradle of Palestine nationalism, supported by the enthusiasm of a local élite open to change, industrialization, trade and commerce.

These contrasts – social, educational, economic, political – were brought to a crisis by the immediate and overwhelming economic problem: how to balance the economy of a population which did not produce enough for its needs; how to avoid making Israel bear the burden of the occupation; how to prevent the resentment produced by the economic crisis from crystallizing and justifying all the other resentments of an enemy and an occupied territory.

The lack of agricultural income on the West Bank was due mainly to two contradictory factors: one permanent and one conjunctional. First, a small crop per dunam (10 dunams equal 1 hectare) with a correspondingly low income per capita, which made investments for development non-existent, and second, an overproduction of specialized crops for export to Arab countries, which could not be absorbed by local markets. Thus, while there was an acute shortage of wheat and barley, and a lesser shortage of other traditional Arab foodstuffs not produced locally, the summer of 1967 found a surplus of 120,000 tons of highly perishable and unsellable agricultural produce, intended for export to now inaccessible markets. There were some 55,000 tons of watermelons and honeydew melons, 21,000 tons of grapes, 22,000 of tomatoes, 9,000 of olives, 5,000 of plums, 4,000 of cucumbers – which Transjordan and other Arab states could absorb but which Israel could make no use of.

A surplus on this scale created two big problems for the Israeli authorities: first, a shortage of money due to the unsold surpluses; and second, a severe reduction of capital in an economy already disrupted by the war, in which the masses of unemployed Arabs were the most fertile recruiting ground for guerrilla activities.

The two solutions found during the summer of 1967 were purely accidental. One consisted of at least a million Israeli customers – 60 per cent of the total population – who poured into the Old City of Jerusalem and the other main towns of the occupied territories, in a wild reaction to the political claustrophobia with which they had been living for the previous twenty years. They bought everything, from agricultural products to baby powder imported by the Jordanian authorities from communist China; from wooden baskets to Bedouin sandals; from old coffee mugs to Arab stamps.[13] While government bank officials were uncertain about the rate of exchange to fix between the Israeli, Jordanian and Egyptian currencies, and the Ministry of Agriculture was submerged by inquiries from Israeli farmers and farming organizations, rightly concerned about the dangers of penetration by cheaper Arab agricultural products into the Israeli market, the citizens of the State (including farmers) poured some thirty-five million Israeli pounds (ten million dollars) into the hands of the inhabitants of the occupied territories, priming the revival of the local economy, supplying part of the cash to replace that impounded by Jordanian banks in Amman, providing a running capital which the Israeli Government would never have been able to mobilize, much less distribute efficiently.

The second, and far more effective, improvised solution, was the crossing of the shallow fords of the River Jordan by Arab farmers with the tacit consent of the military authorities on both sides of the river.[14] In this way, the unsold surpluses of vegetables found their unorthodox – and later official – way into Transjordan, where a population traditionally dependent on West Bank agriculture, and now swelled by 200,000 refugees, clamoured for food. The result was the disposal of agricultural surpluses outside the Israeli market, despite the existing state of war.

These solutions were improvised and depended on shifting political and psychological conditions upon which the Israeli authorities could not rely. By the middle of July, the problem of how to activate West Bank Arab agriculture had become a paramount problem for the Israeli Government – paramount also because 50 per cent of the West Bank population were farmers, and an additional 20 per cent lived on agricultural services.

The problem of modernizing a traditional agriculture

To the men in charge of the economy and development of the West Bank, the tasks to be achieved were clearly definable:
(a) They had to increase the agricultural production of the occupied areas in order to diminish their economic reliance on imported food;
(b) they had to do so by reducing at the same time the existing crops, which were mainly intended for export to the Arab States, because of the insecurity of the commercial routes into the Arab States through the Jordan River;
(c) they had to achieve both the increase of the new agricultural production and the decrease of the old one without arousing the hostility of either the Israeli farmers (who feared Arab competi-

tion) or the Arab farmers (who regarded the switching of West Bank agricultural production as a step towards integration into the Israeli economy).

The two problems stated in (c) above were typical problems of modernization. They were dealt with by a combination of authority, prestige and personal diplomacy.

'Prestige' was mainly directed towards the Arabs, whereas 'authority' was required to withstand Israeli pressure groups which strongly opposed any development – especially agricultural development – in the occupied territories.

It soon became clear, however, to the men asked to deal with the problem of agricultural development in the occupied territories, that they had little possibility of doing their job just by issuing orders. If they were to issue orders, these would simply be disobeyed. Even if they had been obeyed, there was no way of checking how they were executed, since there were few Arab experts available. To train such manpower would have taken years, and to use Israelis was an impractical proposition. In the first place, even if Israelis had been available, it was unlikely that they would willingly work to develop an agriculture which they regarded as competitive – and enemy-owned at that. Further, even without all these obstacles, the physical presence of Israeli experts on the West Bank would have looked like colonialism; this, in turn, would have given the Arab guerrillas excellent opportunities to kill Israeli experts in the fields, thus using the agricultural development scheme as a stepping stone to consolidate their prestige. The Army could not guarantee the security of such experts, and if it had tried to do so, the psychological impact on the farmers would have been ruinous. The problem, therefore, had to be solved by other, indirect and – even more important – exclusively Arab means.

The innovators

To any expert in development and extension agriculture in underdeveloped countries, the problem might have seemed insoluble. To the man who was given the job of tackling it, it was a long-awaited opportunity to apply some basic ideas in development which he had acquired during a period spent in agricultural development work in Israel and in Africa.

Eitan Israely was born in 1934, in Israel. He grew up on a *Moshav*, served in the Pioneer Units of the Israeli Army, received his M.Sc. in Agriculture from the Hebrew University of Jerusalem, worked on the development of the Arava Region, and spent four years in Africa as an agricultural expert. He was thirty-three years old in 1967 when he was called up for active service as a Brigade Operations Officer on the outbreak of the Six-Day War, with the rank of captain. His brigade was faced with numerous civilian problems resulting from the Jordanian defeat on the West Bank, and he volunteered to organize a rescue scheme for stranded animals in the Tulkarm area. This was the natural reaction of a farmer, shocked by the suffering of livestock in an agricultural area where the shock of the war, combined with a disrupted water supply and the summer heat, seemed to cause more lasting damage to the population than the military operation itself.

This rescue scheme for livestock was the first link in a chain of actions and reactions which eventually made Captain Israely the virtual head of all agricultural development on the West Bank. The decision to appoint him to this post was to a considerable extent fortuitous. He happened to be available for a task which no one else in his brigade was either trained for or particularly anxious to assume. It is quite possible that sooner or later Eitan Israely would have been called upon to deal with the problem of agricultural development on the West Bank, since he was particularly well qualified for the task. However, the fact that he was the first person to engage in this task, that he started it while still in the Army – with wide authority and no strings attached by his Brigade Commander, who knew next to nothing about agriculture – undoubtedly helped him to establish the patterns of action which would later be developed.

When Eitan Israely was first put in charge of the agriculture of Samaria, and later of the West Bank he had not formulated any precise, socio-economic model of development, though he did have some very personal ideas about the strategy and tactics of agricultural development in a traditional society. This strategy was based on two observations: first, innovation is diffused by a process of imitation, going from bottom to top, and not by a process of change proceeding from top to bottom in the social cycle. Second, since initiative is closely linked to personal economic incentives, and since economic incentives are closely connected with the feeling of the people affected by price variations that they themselves can somehow control the mechanism of these variations, it is essential that any innovation in a traditional society be linked with the economic mechanism of the traditional markets, and not of foreign markets.

In West Africa, where Eitan Israely worked for four years, he was struck by the fact that farmers in a traditional agricultural society feared development, because innovations always required specialization of techniques or crops which could not be under the direct control of the farmers. Such societies, in any case, tend to organize their production in the most autarchic way possible, because of a lack of capital combined with their fear of economic disruption due to pests, drought, or an excess of rain at the wrong time. Where even the simplest machinery was involved in innovation – such as an iron plough – it required for its maintenance and repair the cooperation of a production market or a foreign technology which the farmer felt was not dependable. The wooden plough, though less efficient, was always locally produced and available, and thus it earned an attachment despite its obvious shortcomings.

The same seemed to be true for crops: agricultural products which could be bought or sold on a local, traditional market, no matter how primitive and unorganized, offered more security than those which had to be sold on distant, foreign markets, processed by foreign, even though well-intentioned, people, and dependent on a system of credits brought about by financial and social denominators alien to people in the traditional society.

As for tactics, Eitan Israely was a firm believer in the fact that bureaucracy generates bureaucracy according to a logic of its own and not necessarily according to the needs of the situation. His idea of bureaucracy in the field of development was based on the simplistic principle that there is a direct link between the energy produced by an organization, and the size of its staff. The more numerous the personnel, the greater the amount of energy which will be absorbed by the organization itself in order to exist, and the less availaible for outside work. He also felt that in the field of development there were no real experts, since no one could claim professional experience in activities linked to so many non-professional variables – social problems, psychological reactions, metaphysical interpretations of natural phenomena, etc., and therefore a programme director should worry less about the technical proficiency of his field experts than about the amount of time they spent in the fields. In terms of operational bureaucratic structures, this meant that one or two men should be subtracted from the planned establishment for any development programme, so that people would always be busy doing other (non-available) people's jobs instead of worrying about their position within the organization.

With these ideas in mind, Eitan Israely started organizing the transformation of West Bank agriculture from a traditional production system to a highly sophisticated modernized one, capable of competing on equal terms with Israeli agriculture, despite the latter's technological and organizational lead of at least thirty years. Three years later, when he left to take up the post of Assistant Director-General in the Israeli Ministry of Agriculture, he had realized most of the task he set himself in October, 1967. What is even more remarkable is that an original model of development evolved in the process, which I call 'the Eitan model', both for convenience and because of the part played by Eitan Israely in developing it. A few words of explanation, however, are needed to set the model in its correct perspective and proportions.

First, the 'Eitan Model' was never a theoretical concept, translated from blueprints to practice. It was a flexible system of field practices, applied in a non-systematic way by people who were learning as they went along. Second, the previous experience in cooperation techniques of the Israeli officials responsible for developing West Bank agriculture was more negative than positive. They knew what they should not do rather than what they should do. Finally, this model – one should perhaps call it an 'experiment' – was the outcome of no single person's efforts, but rather of a group of dedicated men, passionately attached to their new responsibility, in which they saw both a personal and a national challenge. They worked without definite plans, but with a few clear goals in mind, acting both as an operative team and a think-as-you-go command group. This group had at its disposal the cooperation of plenty of Israeli experts in development, as well as well-staffed and organized specialist offices and research institutes in Israel. The need to keep the number of Israelis working in the occupied areas to a minimum – for political and security reasons – turned out to be a blessing in disguise. Bureaucracy was kept to a minimum, and the entire operation was finally carried out with only six persons. They had all had experience in agricultural work in developing countries, and one had specialized in the development of the Arab village in Israel. The ratio was one Israeli to many thousands of Arabs engaged in agriculture. This meant not only that there was a total absence of any visible 'foreign' executive structure, but also that because of the immensity of the job for which each Israeli expert was supposed to be responsible, there was no time for internal bureaucratic work.

Apart from Eitan Israely himself (who, as we have already said, had had lengthy experience in the *Moshav* movement in Israel, and as an agricultural expert in West Africa), there was Amos Rafman, Yoel Pruginin, Ze'ev Ben Herut, Yaakov Katzir, and David Gefen, and Ygael Tsur, all working in the field.

One might, however, place the impact of their work in the proper perspective, i.e. in the historical and social context of the West Bank economy, which in many respects is a special case. The West Bank Arabs have had almost uninterrupted experience of foreign – or at least non-local – administration: first the Turks, then the British, then the Jordanians, and now the Israelis. Although they disliked the Israelis more than any of the others, they did not react against them with the vigour which might have been expected. This facilitated the task of the new military administration. Socially, the Palestinians are one of the most open societies of the Middle East, and perhaps of the whole Mediterranean area, accustomed to receiving and absorbing foreign influences. On the other hand, they form a homogeneous group on the West Bank some 600,000 strong, enough to make any experience in the modernization of their economy relevant, but perhaps not enough to permit general conclusions to be drawn. Finally, the contiguity of the West Bank with Israel (in many cases villages had been divided by the 1948–67 armistice lines) brought the West Bank Arabs into close contact with the Israeli model of a developing society. They could not, therefore, avoid – and did not try to avoid – making constant comparisons between the two ways of life, a situation which increased the impact of the agricultural development initiated by the military administration.

For all these reasons the situation on the West Bank could not easily be reproduced elsewhere. However, it provided fertile ground for a small group of men entirely dedicated to their ideas of technical cooperation.

The one thing which all members of the group had in common – and from every point of view this was an asset to them – was the prestige of the military status under which they operated. It was not a position of authority, since the very temporary situation of an occupying army did not permit them to rely on any clear-cut government policy. But as long as they improvised, as long as their initiatives did not meet with official opposition in Israel, they had the advantage of being able to take quick decisions, unfettered by bureaucratic red tape. In their work, which was conceived initially as an operation to restore normalcy to the agricultural life of the occupied areas in the quickest possible time, they were given – or, more accurately, they took – a free hand. They were not, after all, regular soldiers, but civilians working within a military government which wanted to be connected as little as possible with the civilian administration of the Arabs. They acted as a disciplined team within, but not dependent on, an administration which had no clear ideas or plans about what should be done on the West Bank in the sphere of agricultural production. All that the military and civilian authorities wanted was that production should continue, that it should not create financial problems in marketing, that it should not require the presence of many Israelis in the occupied areas, or investment of Israeli capital over the 'green line' separating Israel from the former Jordanian area.

Each of the five experts in Israely's team thus rapidly became almost an independent 'boss' in his own area. They reported loosely and informally to the head of the team who had, in fact, now replaced the former Jordanian Director-General for Agriculture and transferred the seat of the supreme agricultural authority of the West Bank Arabs from Amman to the West Bank itself.

First decisions

From the very beginning of their work in the occupied areas, the Israeli authorities found themselves confronted with a situation which offered both opportunities and obstacles to change and innovation. The centralization of the Jordanian bureaucracy in Amman, for example, was a situation which unexpectedly played into the hands of the Military Government. The men responsible for West Bank agriculture prior to the Six-Day War were in Amman, and all decisions had to be referred to them by their West Bank officials. Quite apart from the natural feelings of frustration which were a permanent undercurrent among West Bank Arabs, this situation made it practically impossible for them to reach executive positions as long as they lived on the West Bank. The Israeli military administration, merely by asking the local, ex-Jordanian officials to take decisions previously taken only in Amman, promoted these same officials to a status of greater authority and local autonomy. The physical detachment of the West Bank from the East Bank, in fact, created bureaucratic vacancies which offered the local officials chances of promotion which they were unlikely to have had under the Jordanian régime.

At the beginning of the Israeli presence, the staff of the agricultural departments amounted to about 200 people. Sixty more specialists were added during 1968 and 1969, recruited mainly among students trained in the Egyptian universities, none of whom, however, had had any experience in modern agriculture. In 1971, all the 260 agricultural officers, including directors of five experimental stations and of three regional offices, were West Bank residents.

Far more important to the Israelis than the structure of the former Jordanian agricultural bureaucracy was the structure and level of the agriculture itself. The Israelis were surprised by the intensity, dedication and results of the agricultural work of West Bank farmers. This was probably one of the most flourishing Arab areas in the Middle East, in which olive and fruit trees, vegetables, tobacco, citrus, bananas (in Jericho) and grapes were successfully grown. Cultivation methods may have been less advanced than in Israel but there was no question about the potential skill of the farmers or their willingness to improve their traditional agriculture. There was no need for the Israeli Administration to fan their desire for improvement, but rather to find ways of channelling it into improved and reoriented fields of production, such as cotton, or new types of vegetables, and into modernization. In this sense, there was a sincere desire on the part of the Arab farmers to learn from the Israelis, and the main question was how they could do so without creating the impression of cooperation with the enemy. As early as July 1968, one of the Arab District Agricultural Directors, a graduate of the University of California Faculty of Agriculture, said to a Jewish journalist (*The Jewish Observer & Middle East Review*, 12.7.68): 'We would like complete autonomy to deal with our farm problems, but meanwhile we would appreciate all useful advice and help from the Israelis. We hope to double the yield of every dunam and crop in a very short period.'*

A third element favourable to the Israeli policy of agricultural development in the occupied areas was the structure of the Arab agriculture itself. An area of 2,715,000 dunams of cultivated land was split up into 58,700 individual farms. This was, of course, a great fragmentation of agricultural property, but on the other hand it meant that there were very few latifundia, and there were a lot of farmers who could, if they were induced to adopt modern, intensive agricultural systems, very quickly raise the whole standard of West Bank agriculture.

Last, but not least, of the potentially positive elements for the new Israeli administration, was a network of cooperative enterprises which the former Jordanian administration had done much to support and develop in the whole Hashemite territory.† This network had grown from 40 cooperative enterprises in 1950 to 707 in 1966, with a total affiliation of 43,058 members. The great majority were simple credit societies, supported by the Government, which provided farmers with small loans. When the Israelis arrived on the West Bank they made an effort to keep the local cooperatives going. They succeeded with a few commercial cooperatives (mainly for the export of agricultural produce to the Arab States), and cooperative oil presses. Most of the others stopped

*I am grateful to Mr G. Weigert, who allowed me to read the draft of his book *Arabs & Israelis: Life Together*, from which I draw many factual details on Arab agriculture in the West Bank.

†For a detailed comparative study of Arab cooperatives in Israel and on the West Bank see G. Weigert, *Hatnua Hashitufit e Yehuda, Hashomron veRetzuat Aza*, (The Cooperative Movement in Judea, Samaria and the Gaza Strip), Mimeograph, 1971, from which most of the information on this specific subject has been drawn.

functioning as soon as they lost contact with the central cooperative offices in Amman, but during the years in which they did function, they had helped to inculcate into at least some of the Arab farmers the idea of cooperation.[15] If, therefore, West Bank agriculture could modernize itself, the cooperative experience should also be able to help it integrate into the highly developed Israeli agriculture. The vital question in the initial stage was how to transform these potentials into facts; how to activate through new energy coming from outside a social 'engine' which was certainly strong but which was constructed for a different type of operation.

However, the number of obstacles to the realization of the Israeli administration's policy in the field of agricultural development seemed at the time to be more numerous and formidable than the potentially positive factors just described. One specific obstacle was that it was extremely dangerous for an Arab official to take initiatives which might single him out in the eyes of the occupied population. Anything which he did together with the Israelis might be interpreted as collaboration, and this was particularly true in the case of planning.

Planning was indispensable for the reorganization of the local agriculture, but to work out a budget a year in advance, or to plan the revision of cultures to fit in with opportunities offered by the Israeli market, or, again, to plan to export produce to Europe instead of to the Arab countries, might well be interpreted not as a technical operation but as a highly political and anti-patriotic action facilitating the enemy occupation.

Another, no less important, problem connected with the Arab agricultural bureaucracy, was of a social nature. For a senior Jordanian official to go out personally and supervise the work of small or medium farmers meant a loss of prestige. They did their work in offices, to which notables had easy access while farmers were either afraid or too shy to call on the officials. In most cases they would not have known what to say even if they had gone there. The lower officials worked in the field, but mostly as specialists and not as general agronomists. This restricted their field activities, since the small and medium farmers had mixed farms with little specialization.

One of the first decisions taken by the new Director of Agriculture was, therefore, to reorganise the structure of agricultural administration on the West Bank. Figure 2 shows how this Department was organized under the Jordanians who had, in fact, built up their agricultural bureaucracy on the British model established almost forty years earlier by the Mandatory Administration. The main Jordanian innovation was dictated by political and not by technical considerations. The Jordanian administration resided in Amman and not in Jerusalem. The British Mandatory Department of Agriculture was thus moved from the Arab sector of Palestine to Amman, with all the main sections, Veterinary, Forestry, Water, etc. The three Districts of Nablus, Jerusalem and Hebron were left with little executive authority, all decisions being referred to Amman. This, incidentally, had some important side effects. For example, since some of the higher officials residing in Amman were recruited from the Transjordanian population and not from the Palestinian – or at least, not from the West Bank – population, they had few direct personal ties with the farmers across the River Jordan. Furthermore, many administrative posts were given to people with university degrees in agriculture, acquired abroad, sometimes in other Arab countries, but more often in Europe or America. They may have possessed a theoretical knowledge of agricultural problems but they had very little practical experience in their own country. The Israelis claim – though this is, of course, a matter of speculation – that they were usually less competent than some of the junior Arab agricultural officials of the West Bank who, despite their lack of university degrees, knew their jobs from their own direct experience with local agriculture.

For the rest, the Jordanians more or less maintained the organization which the British had left to them. This organization was based on a combination of functional and geographical departments, the functional ones being considered more important in status than the geographical ones. There was a Department of Forestry, a Water Department, a Department for Agricultural Extension, and a Veterinary Department, all of which had their own specialized representatives at each lower echelon of the organization. Then there were Branch Directors, whose job was to coordinate the work of the specialists in their own particular district. At the farmers' level, this organization produced a number of technical and psychological difficulties.

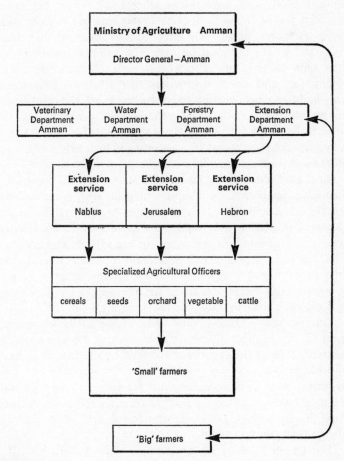

Figure 2

Organization of the Jordan Agricultural Extension service at the time of the Israeli Occupation of the West Bank, June 1967

The big farmers, whenever they needed help or advice from the agricultural administration, went directly to Amman. The resident West Bank agricultural officers, who were not given executive power, found themselves doubly snubbed, both by their superior officers 'beyond the river' (often Transjordanian Bedouin) and by the big local farmers. The local officers defended their white-collar status by sticking to their offices in their towns of residence and issuing instructions to the farmers from there. This had two negative effects: on the one hand, the officials did not go into the fields to look for the farmers' problems, and the small farmers did not usually come to them, either because they were afraid of government officials sitting in their urban offices or, more often, because they did not know what to ask them.

On the other hand, the junior agricultural officials considered themselves specialists, each representing his own branch within the Department itself. For instance, the Agricultural Extension Department, dealing with training and development, was divided according to the various field crops, or branches of agriculture, a situation which made coordination between officials weak, and inter-departmental rivalry strong. To the farmers in the traditional villages, all this meant one thing: the less they had to do with an agricultural official, the safer and the better for them.

Turning from problems connected with the Jordanian agricultural officials to those of transfer of know-how, it became evident that very little of the experience acquired by the Israelis in Arab agriculture inside the State of Israel could be applied to the task of getting West Bank agriculture moving and reoriented. Perhaps the most useful experience was negative, in the sense that in Israel itself the direct linking of Arab with Jewish agricultures had not always been very successful.

The Israeli Minister of Agriculture, Haim Givati, himself a *kibbutz* farmer, implicitly recognized this when he declared at an Agricultural Fair held in Nablus that the rate of increase of agricultural yields on the West Bank (he referred in particular to cereals which had grown sixfold in five years) had been more rapid under Israeli administration than in Israel itself (*The Jerusalem Post*, 16.8.72). The negative results of the direct transfer of methods of development, planning and organization from the Jewish to the Arab economy in Israel, for instance, were evident in the field of cooperative organization. Despite the development of the cooperative movement in Israel and the efforts of the Histadrut (the Israeli Labour Federation) to organize Israeli Arabs into agricultural and other types of cooperative structures, results were extremely poor. In the sphere of marketing of produce, not one of the forty-two Arab cooperatives created in Israel between 1949 and 1952 still existed in 1957, while the four general Arab Agricultural Cooperatives established in 1949 had increased to only ten, twenty years later.

It was imperative, therefore, that an entirely new approach to development should be followed in modernizing West Bank agriculture, different not only from that applied to Jewish and Arab agriculture in Israel, but also from that of the Jordanian Government (and its western experts). It was not a matter of planning – political conditions in 1967 made any long-term planning impossible – but of priming the Arab agricultural 'machine' so that it could catch up with its own potential and resources, and adapt to the trend of modernization born of the new political situation. The priming was carried out by the Israeli administration in stages: First a radical reorganization of the existing agricultural bureaucracy; then the establishment of farmers' committees; and finally, the activation of the new structures with the help of the traditional leadership, which alone could legitimize the acceptance of an imported innovation.

Reorganization of roles

After the Six-Day War, the higher executive echelons of the Jordanian agricultural administration were left beyond the border and the posts of District Offices Director on the West Bank became weakened. One possibility would have been to carry on with the Jordanian system, and to appoint new Heads of Departments and new District Directors within the Ministry of Agriculture in Jerusalem; another to appoint Jewish officials to be in charge of Districts and Departments; a third to promote the junior agricultural officers of the West Bank to greater responsibility. The new administration decided on the last alternative. The hesitation of the Arab agricultural officers to cooperate with the occupying authorities was overcome by stressing their duty to serve their fellow farmers, and by convincing them that cows and fruit recognize seasons and drought but not the colour of flags. Personal pride was also played upon, the local junior experts being made conscious of the chance 'to show the people in Amman' what they were able to do when given the opportunity.

The most important change introduced by the new administration was, however, different in nature. While the Jordanian bureaucratic set-up was left more or less untouched, i.e. the division between functional Departments (Forestry, Veterinary, etc.) was retained, the Extension Department (i.e. the Department for training) which, for the reasons described above, was very much the Cinderella of the agricultural administration in the former set-up, became the main administrative channel through which the new administration decided to work. Field Instructors in this Department, who were also specialized agronomists, were ordered out of their offices and told to spend their time with the farmers in the villages. Their competence was changed from a specialized to a territorial one. Instead of being responsible for a given type of crop, they were made responsible for all agricultural activities in a given area. A certain number of villages, the number varying according to their size, was made the direct responsibility of each officer, whose main duty now consisted of paying regular visits to the village headmen, hearing their complaints, taking down their requests or obtaining statistical information from them which the new Director of Agriculture required to plan his future production policy. A simple but rigorous system of control was established on the activities of these new 'field officers'. Their tours in the villages were to be announced in writing both to the village headmen and to Eitan Israely who always made a point of touring the same areas at the same time, without, however, interfering in the Field Instructors' duties.

The required statistical information soon began to pour in, together with a lot of requests from the farmers. They were directed by the Extension Department Field Officers to the various Departments concerned, as well as to the Director of the Extension Department. The latter was made responsible for the coordination of agricultural activities at his own level, as well as with the District Director to whom he could turn for directives or with complaints. The whole bureaucratic machinery thus became geared to the Agricultural Extension Department, with the help of which the new administration decided to apply its model for development.

Using the services of the Extension Department Field Instructors working within precise territorial limits, a second important decision was taken. Arab agricultural officers were instructed to organize the village farmers into permanent committees whose function would be to present regularly to the occupation authorities, through the new Head of Agricultural Administration, the many problems created by the new situation. It was only natural that these farmers were the most prominent persons, some kind of local agricultural notables and that the 'professional' and 'social' questions were intentionally allowed to mix. In fact, it was the belief of the new heads of West Bank agriculture that it would be impossible to win the confidence and respect of the Arab farmers in the occupied areas, or of their leaders, only on an official level. The delineation of personal relations and common interests outside the field of agriculture was considered an integral part of the desired process of innovation, and the Jewish officials were constantly reminded of this. This, in turn, led to some unexpected situations: for instance, it was to the new Director of Agriculture that Arab farmers first turned with the half-joking suggestion that they should be allowed to ford the River Jordan with unsold agricultural surpluses and make their own private arrangements with the Jordanian soldiers on the other bank, 'provided the Israeli guards would not fire on them while crossing'. The suggestion was taken by Eitan Israely to the Regional Military Commander for approval, and was put into practice without any previous agreement from the political authorities in Jerusalem. When it proved satisfactory, it was given the blessing of the Israeli Government, thus starting a major economic and political revolution in the relations between Israel and Jordan.

However, despite the possible importance of the personal contacts thus established with Arabs in the frame of the farmers' committees, the main idea behind the creation of the committees was neither political nor social, but purely agricultural. It was believed that they could become the main channels through which the occupying authorities hoped to introduce changes into West Bank agriculture.

The new structure was not at the time fully defined: Eytan

Israely and his collaborators were formulating and trying out their ideas as they went along, on the basis of their past experience in Africa. The ideas behind the structures were not original in themselves, nor, at the time, even organic. They formed a cluster of conceptions drawn from different experience, which had the novelty of not having been applied consistently and systematically within a comprehensive frame of a totally controlled development effort.

The significance of establishing committees of agricultural notables

The first idea was that no innovation could be introduced by people from above. It had to mature in the minds of the people who were to adopt it, and the adviser's role was to ensure that the process of maturation be as rapid and as controllable as possible.

The second idea was that no matter how good the innovation, it would not be accepted by the traditional farmers if it had not first received the legitimation of those people who, in that particular field of innovation, represented the accepted and traditional authority capable of producing this legitimation.

The committees of farmers became a fundamental element in the new structure envisaged by the military administration. The major difficulty at the time (late 1967 and early 1968) was to keep them knitted together without their being regarded as an instrument of the conquering power. Afterwards, the committees were urged to deal with matters sometimes remotely connected with agricultural development, such as recommendations for travel permits, import licences, etc., and also with the planning of production and marketing, which implied an Arab acceptance of the Israelis.

The second instrument available to the Israeli innovators was the former Jordanian agricultural officials. Through them, and only through them, could the new Director of Agriculture make contact with farmers and notables. Their authority, however, was limited to their ability to serve as more or less effective channels of information and instruction, between the Israeli agricultural authorities and the village notables or the Arab farmers. The mode of operation at this stage looked rather like a triangle, but it was still static, with little interchange of ideas, impulses or reactions. The only innovation was the creation of the agricultural committees which, for the moment, restricted their activities to formal and rather passive contact with the Israeli authorities, but, in fact, already provided the essential link between two societies operating at different levels of energy.

The activation of the structure

The Israeli administration was aiming at the transformation of the static triangle into an active system of innovation processing. They knew that whatever organization they created for the introduction of changes and innovations, it could not be a hierarchical one, similar to that which had existed (and remained idle) under the Jordanian authorities. This authority, whether efficient or not, was the legal and accepted authority on the West Bank: it could give orders and expect to be obeyed. The Israeli authority, on the other hand, was a foreign one, deeply resented by the population. It would have been only natural that its orders be ignored – especially when natural resistance to change was reinforced by the feeling that passive resistance was patriotic. There was little hope that Israeli suggestions, advice, incentives and so on, in the field of agriculture, could bring results, even if recognized by the Arabs as being worth while, unless the new ideas could be planted in the minds of the local people and develop into an Arab initiative.

For this, an operational structure was needed which would act along the lines of an electrical transformer. It should first bring in the high-tension foreign impulses, then transform them into a lower voltage more acceptable to the local farmers, through an indigenous system of legitimation, and finally make the new current available to the people in such a way that they would be convinced that by switching from traditional to modern agriculture they were not complying with the wishes of the conquerors but following their traditional leaders in an effort of modernization which would help them to oppose more effective resistance to the foreign invaders.

The scheme was put into practice in less than two years of intense manipulation of production techniques, markets and traditional authority.

The manipulation of markets was required as a conditional step

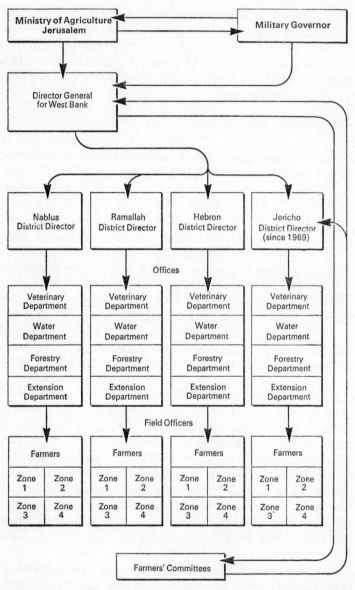

Figure 3

Changes introduced by the Israeli military authorities during summer 1967

to provide for a change in the type of agricultural production. How, for instance, could the farmers be induced to stop growing water melons and switch to tomatoes (which the Israeli industry could absorb and export) without arousing psychological and political resistance. Even if industry in Israel had been interested in purchasing, say, tomatoes, for its own benefit, his African experience had taught Israely the impossibility of ordering a traditional farmer to grow something new. He had to be made willing to make the transition from water melons to export tomatoes, which would entail more involved techniques to protect such crops from blight, and to meet the standards required by industry.

Then there was the political problem of how a new culture, imposed by the occupying authority, however beneficial it might be economically, could be accepted by Arab farmers without the fear of being accused of collaboration with the enemy.

Traditional crops

The solution to this double problem was found in the following way. A careful investigation was carried out in the various areas to establish which crops the Arab farmers had grown prior to the development of water melon and other surplus products for export to the Arab states. It was discovered that all the export crops on the West Bank were comparatively recent and were related to the consumer demand of Palestinians residing in the Arab states, and particularly in the oil sheikhdoms. Simple questionnaires were distributed to the farmers through the Arab agricultural officers, asking what they had cultivated 5, 10 or 15 years previously. In some cases older farmers were eager to volunteer information because they felt that the earlier traditional crops were better and more remunerative than the later, export crops (such as water melons). After this it was easy to establish a list of traditional crops and to select from the list those items for which the Israeli market could offer a remunerative price. The choice finally fell on sesame and chick peas, used by both Arabs and Jews in their diet, with the former even being processed for export by Israeli sweet factories. The only snag was the low price of these items, due to the ease with which they could be imported across the River Jordan to the West Bank.

A tax was therefore imposed on sesame and chick peas imported from Jordan (IL 450 per ton on sesame and IL 200 per ton on chick peas), and this sent the price of these items in the West Bank and in Israel sky-high. This helped to save dollars for the Israeli economy, but it immediately created a strong demand for the local product in the Arab market, which the traditional farming experience of the Arabs met with no difficulty. The switch from a type of crop saleable only on Arab markets outside Israel, to one which could be sold locally in the farmers' traditional market, was thus achieved without effort and with no psychological resistance. This made it possible for the Arab farmers on the West Bank – or at least some of them – to continue receiving a basic income, despite the growing difficulty of exporting agricultural produce to Arab countries east of the Jordan. Moreover, it was a direct application of the principle held by the new directors of West Bank agriculture, namely, that any change must take place as far as possible within the framework of the traditional economic market of a traditional agricultural society, in order not to destroy the accepted economic habits of that same society.

The investigation into the types of agricultural crops previously raised by Arab farmers on the West Bank, and the statistical information collected by the Junior Agricultural Officers of the Extension Department in the areas under their control, established the exact areas of other cultivation – for instance, of tomatoes. There was a great demand in Israel for these crops, provided they could meet the requirements of the Israeli food industries in quality, quantity and delivery times.

A new market for old crops

At this point it was suggested to farmers, through the Arab Field Officers of the Extension Department, that they try out new varieties of the crops they were already growing, explaining that this could bring them a higher income. Great care was taken to avoid proposing the introduction of crops which would sell well on the Israeli market (for instance, cucumbers and haricot beans) but which were not in current use on the West Bank. The assumption was that if Arab farmers were asked to introduce new crops the project would probably fail. Either the novelty itself would arouse problems with which the farmers would not be able to cope and the inevitable failures would increase the general resistance to the innovation, or the new and remunerative crops might prove a success. In that case, they would inevitably create jealousy and, since they were intended for sale on the Israeli market or to Israeli industry, those farmers who for one reason or another had not produced the new crops might spread the idea that those growing the crops were cooperating with the enemy. No amount of persuasion or technical aid would then be able to overcome such a non-technical obstacle.

The introduction of new varieties of existing crops was clearly intended to provide agricultural supplies for the Israeli food industry and to detach West Bank Arab farmers from their dependence on Arab markets beyond the border. This aim was achieved by an indirect approach, which consisted first of strengthening the economic links of the Arab farmers with Arab markets beyond the border, and only later loosening them. The logic of this policy was based on the principle of legitimization of innovation by the traditional indigenous authority as a necessary step for the diffusion (through imitation) of the innovation. Only later, when the innovation had been fully accepted by the farmers, was it possible to deal with it in accordance with the general policy of the occupying authorities. Thus, it was suggested to Arab farmers who were already growing tomatoes, that they try out the San Marzano variety developed in Italy, which had a higher dry-matter content than their traditional variety. The San Marzano tomato is one of the tomatoes grown in Israel and treated by the Israeli canning industry. It was suggested to Arab farmers that they try it out only for export to Arab markets, in view of the fact that the lower water content made it travel well in hot climates. The success of the San Marzano tomatoes grown on the West Bank at the Kuwait market (largely controlled by Palestinians) was beyond all expectations. The Arab farmers were asked by their own exporters to increase production of the new vegetable as much as possible because of its high return. The Arab farmers readily agreed, turning to the Agricultural Officers of the Extension Department for advice and proper seeds. They were given both, with the additional promise that any quantity of San Marzano tomatoes not exported to Kuwait or elsewhere in the Arab countries, would be absorbed by the Israeli canning industry at fixed prices.

The same policy was followed for other crops, for instance, the Black Beauty variety of aubergine, widely exported by Israel to Europe. It worked smoothly and to the satisfaction of everyone concerned. It even had its humorous side, with some of the more nationalistic Arab farmers on the West Bank boasting that the top quality vegetables were for the Arab tables, and the poor quality for the 'Israeli dogs', that is, for the canning industry.

It took very little time, however, for the entire new West Bank surplus yield to be switched solely to the Israeli market. The political situation between the Arab countries and Israel, and the constant fear of finding the bridges over the Jordan closed for indefinite periods, made the Arab farmers willing to sell their agricultural produce to Israel and Europe. Today it is impossible to distinguish between a Jewish or a West Bank Arab-grown aubergine on sale in Hamburg. Their quality and the price they fetch is identical, and the process of diffusion of the innovation irreversible.

Experiments

Not all the innovations brought about by the Israelis in West Bank agriculture, spread so effectively, though the methods adopted were always founded on the same principle: diffusion of change by traditional legitimization from the indigenous authority. The reduction of areas growing traditional crops, such as sesame (which the Israelis themselves promoted at an earlier stage, as mentioned earlier), chick peas or water melons, is an illuminating example. The method employed was the following. The new Director of Agriculture informally asked his senior Arab agricultural officers to choose from among their families or friends those who, as farmers, had the highest social standing in a particular area. Among these, a second selection established the names of those who owned fields at such 'strategic' points as near a main road, or in the centre of a village. These 'notable' farmers were invited, together with anyone else who wished to attend, to visit Israeli agricultural areas for demonstration days organized by the Israeli Ministry of Agriculture, to show what had been achieved by the ultra-modern Jewish agriculture. These trips always aroused great interest among the West Bank farmers, and led to inevitable feelings of jealousy of Jewish achievements.

Early in the winter of 1968 the Arab agricultural officers were called in and asked to approach their 'selected' relatives with the following proposition. If they agreed to allow the agricultural officers to establish an experimental demonstration project in a prominent location, visible to the largest possible number of passers by, the Israeli agricultural authorities would provide the Arab officers with all the necessary experience, instruction and extra expenses needed to demonstrate to their relatives and friends that, given the right conditions, anybody with some agricultural experience could do as well as the Israelis. The local farmers still remained responsible for the normal agricultural work, in the experimental plots, to avoid creating the impression that the initiative was a government one, to be considered as outside the sphere of a normal farm undertaking.

The feeling of national pride, which could have proved an obstacle to innovation by the Israelis, was thus used, in combination with the genuine professional ambition of the Arab agricultural officers, to promote changes in traditional West Bank agriculture.

Great care was taken, however, not to extend the facilities to all the farmers at once, but only to the selected Arab notables. The obstacle to be overcome was a matter of status, not of technique. The aim at this stage was *first* the legitimization of the innovation by the traditional social authority of the Arab village, and *second* the demonstration of one system's superiority over the other. Thus, early in 1968, the demonstration fields were restricted in number and areas – not more than a dozen or so in all.

By the summer of 1968, the difference between the produce and the cash return of the traditional and the demonstration fields was so evident that the West Bank agricultural officers were besieged with requests from notables and ordinary farmers to give them the same instruction in the new agricultural techniques as had so far only been given to the officers' closer relatives. Furthermore, the success of the demonstration fields was a source of both professional pride and enhanced status for the agricultural officers themselves. As far as their relatives were concerned, their one request was to extend the area of the demonstration fields – particularly since they had incurred no expense for the demonstration. They enjoyed the sweetness of a success which –

in terms of contrasting political psychology – proved the ability of the conquered to be as good as, if not better than, the conqueror. After all, they had used their own abilities.

The institutionalization of innovation

By 1969, the legitimization of the agricultural innovation by the traditional West Bank society was an accomplished fact. The operative model used by the Israeli administration ceased to be a static 'triangle' and became a dynamic 'transformer' of impulses and a working system for controllable legitimization. The farmers' committees, which had acted during most of the previous fifteeen months mainly as passive channels of liaison with the occupying Israeli authorities, were not transformed into committees which discussed with the Arab agricultural officers the best way of enlarging the scope and areas of the new agricultural methods. The model, by the end of 1969, was as Figure 4.

The main change was in the dynamics, in both senses, namely, that the impulses of innovation provided by the Israelis were now reciprocated by strong impulses emanating from the Arab farmers. The latter requested innovation, but also used their committees to discuss ways and means of adapting these innovations to the local situation.

No less important was the question of the appointment of local farmers to the committees, the struggle for local influence and authority – in which the Israelis made a point of never interfering.

Despite all these new ideas and activities, however, the whole system remained part and parcel of a traditional economy and a traditional society, the leadership of which was to a large extent in the hands of those people who had higher social status, and not necessarily those who had higher intelligence or more initiative. The Israeli agricultural planners found themselves caught by the process of modernization that they had initiated and found it less necessary to remain in contact with the farmers' committees. Furthermore, the structure of Arab society on the West Bank was changing so rapidly as a result of the occupation, that being in contact with the notables might have been a political choice, and possibly not the most intelligent one from the Israeli point of view.

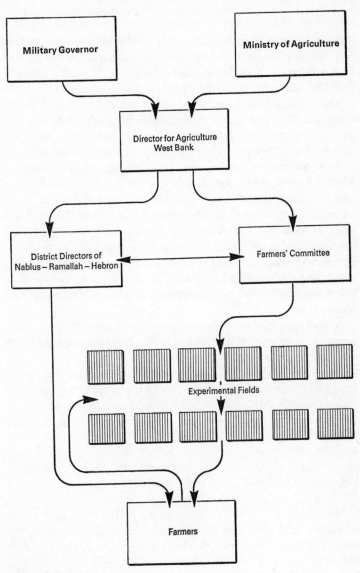

Figure 4
'Eitan Model', winter 1968

The effects of innovation

After two years of occupation, several inevitable changes had, in fact, taken place in the Arab society. Some part of the landed élite had left the West Bank, though far fewer than those who had fled from the areas occupied by Israel in 1948.

The rise in labourers' wages – due to the increased demand for manpower in Israel – made it impossible for the large landowners to continue employing labourers on the old production system. On the one hand, therefore, the new economic situation forced land-owners to improve and modernize their agricultural methods. More frequently, however, it was the small and medium farmers who now found themselves with additional capital, brought home as wages by members of the family employed in Israel. It was these small farmers, who were anxious to make the best use of their holdings, and whose families were becoming familiar with the Israeli way of life and production methods, who most eagerly sought the advice of agricultural officers, and were most ready to invest money in the modernization of their agricultural processes.

A new type of farmer began to emerge on the West Bank, a farmer who at some time had had agricultural holdings, and who was now in possession of some spare capital. During the first and second years of the Israeli occupation, all this spare cash went on food and amenities for families. But by the end of 1969 the value of agricultural production on the West Bank had risen 31 per cent. This meant that the area had become more self-sufficient and was even accumulating capital, thanks to the wages of the 50,000 workers who travelled daily to work in the Israeli zone. It also meant that the West Bank economy was becoming increasingly independent of Jordan and other Arab countries, thus reversing the situation which had existed two years earlier [16].

The political and social implications of this profound trans-formation have yet to be studied and its consequences form the subject of heated debate among both Israelis and Arabs. We shall not enter into this very complex aspect of the problem. We are, however, convinced that whatever the final outcome of Israel's administration of the West Bank, it can already provide ample material for the student of technical cooperation and agricultural development.

The first indisputable result of this administration is the accomplishment in a very short period of time – three years – of an agricultural revolution of major proportions in the entire West Bank society, *without any land reform.*

Land reform might have been a better and more radical way to change the socio-economic structures of the West Bank, but it presupposes some clear political ideology on the part of the Israeli authorities towards the Arabs in the occupied areas. Such an ideology, though possibly supported by some minor leftist groups, lacked weight in the Government's political plans and policies for

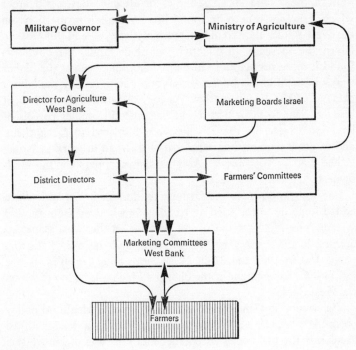

Figure 5
'Eitan Model', 1969

the West Bank. But even had the government in Jerusalem held such views, it is doubtful whether it would have been able to apply them at all, in view of its declared policy to maintain only a temporary presence in most of the Arab populated areas conquered during the Six-Day War.[17] What, in fact, did happen was that the increased yield per dunam brought about by the agricultural innovations introduced by the new administration, and rapidly diffused thanks to the legitimization of the traditional authority, meant an ever higher income for West Bank farmers. In the case of big Arab landlords, who used to have sharecroppers cultivating their land (one of the rooted social scourges of all underdeveloped areas which, however was to be found in very limited proportions on the West Bank), they found increasingly less value in this system. Given the increased productivity of their lands, the landlords found it more profitable to hire day labourers, even at the higher wages brought about by the Israeli occupation and by the labour demand of the Israeli market. As for the farmers themselves, it became clear to them that it was better to till smaller parcels of land intensively, as the Israelis were prepared to teach them, and to grow the new industrial crops, or to go to work in Israel, rather than to continue working as sharecroppers for the landowners.

For both landowners and farmers, modernization of agriculture added impetus to the existing trend to break away from the old system. The fact that the use of manure on the West Bank increased in three years by 500 per cent, and the use of tractors (from 150 in 1967 to 532 in 1970) more than threefold, is one indication of the extent of the changes which are taking place on the West Bank.

The second indisputable result of the Israeli agricultural policy on the West Bank is the activation of a traditional leadership to accelerate the process of acceptance and diffusion of innovation. The conditions existing on the West Bank were clearly very peculiar ones. Arab farmers, despite their political opposition to the Israeli, were most eager to learn from him and – in the field of agriculture, at all events – had a deep respect for Israeli technical and organizational skills. Furthermore, in the development of West Bank agriculture there was no need to start from scratch:

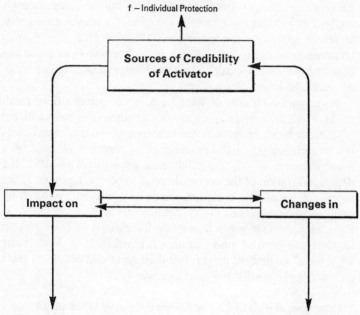

Ability to Fulfil Requests
a – Controlled Goods
b – Transportation
c – Supply of Irrigation Water
d – Opening of New Markets
e – Issue of Travel Permits
f – Individual Protection

Sources of Credibility of Activator

Impact on

Changes in

1. Environment
   Revival of old crops
   Increase old crops with new techniques
   Use of old crops on new markets
   Transfer of know-how (demonstration plots)
2. Men
   Handling of legitimizing élites
   Overcoming of psychological resistance
   Prevention of friction with foreign authority
   Training

Economics
Social structure
Political structure

Figure 6

it could be founded on a considerable amount of actual and potential skill and resources. Yet one could point to many similar situations – for instance the case of agriculture in Sicily, even in the citrus groves in which the introduction of new, imported techniques did not produce equally vast and quick results.

The model which we have tried to describe was not a comprehensive agricultural development plan, but a comprehensive method of priming the untapped energies of a traditional society. It served to handle the legitimate traditional élite of a farming community within its own setting, in such a way as to make this élite operate – so to speak – as a transformer of one type of socio-economic 'voltage' into another.

In the particular case of West Bank Arab society a third result – which will, however, require much more time to be substantiated – seems to be an increase in the influence of the traditional élites in the early stages of the modernization process, followed by a rapid decrease in this same influence as a direct result of the depersonalization of the economic process of development. If the repercussions of this evolution can in any way be measured by political standards, then the 1972 municipal elections of the West Bank may provide some interesting indications of the direction in which the wind of modernization is blowing. In these elections 14 of the 23 incumbent mayors lost their seats, and out of 192 seats on municipal councils, 109 went to newcomers.

How does all this fit into our general theory? Obviously Eitan's group, as Israelis promoting agricultural development in the occupied West Bank, were foreigners, by their own as well as by native standards. Their actions were transformed into strangers' actions (in Simmel's sense) the moment that (a) they submitted their innovations for the judgement and approval of the native authorities for legitimation, and (b) they did so in full and reasoned observance of the proper 'etiquette'. This required that not only had traditional legitimation of innovation to be sought, but that it be clear to both the legitimating authorities and to the masses that this was being done in the proper form. This involved giving the customary personal respect and attention to the indigenous authority and establishing relations with this same authority in fields which went far beyond official or technical matters.

Admittedly the Arab agricultural notables were not political authorities. They held little political power under the Jordanians and even less under the Israeli military administration. But they remained in full possession of the 'imitative hold', all the more so because of the confused political situation. Furthermore, they could be 'activated in their own setting', because the initiative for such activation came from very few people and was exerted directly also on very few people, on a carefully chosen basis of micro-cooperation.

Despite the obvious differences, the process of agricultural development on the occupied West Bank of the Jordan was inspired, for better or for worse, by the same logic as the story, *The Bridge over the River Kwai*. The bridge, created by one type of situational authority and order, becomes the source of another type of situational authority and order – or disorder – once it has been completed.

The moral of such development cannot be judged except in terms of relative values, unless one believes that development and economic progress are a good in themselves. If there is a moral in the examples of micro-cooperation which we have attempted to discuss in these pages, it is a very simple one. To innovate in a society different from one's own, one should not dismiss but rather first identify and then make use of that authority which can legitimate change and that 'imitative pull', which can diffuse it.

Conclusion

The cases of aid-to-development described in the preceding chapters – Madagascar, Peru, Afghanistan and the West Bank of the Jordan – are far apart in terms of time, geography, social and political setting. But these very differences stress the element common to the four cases – as in fact, common to all cases of transculturation – namely, the relevant relationship between the alien carriers of innovation and the traditional élites, which encourages the legitimization of the innovation and helps its *in loco* diffusion.

To stress this relationship does not mean to equate the complex process of transculturation and modernization with the role of the innovator and that of the traditional élites. Neither is it being claimed that this process can be better understood by looking only through the keyhole of the man-in-the-middle. Considering, however, the difficulties of the socio-psychological adaptation of men to situations of constant change – the trickiest of the many critical variables characterizing the process of modernization – it seems important to find a way of submitting this socio-psychological variable to some kind of empirical verification.

One way which has been suggested in this book is to study the specific relationship between the innovation carriers and the traditional élites, a relationship which can serve to legitimize activities. My thesis is not only that this relationship is present in every process of transculturation, but that its study would help to establish the distinction between the *positive innovator*, represented by the stranger, and the *negative innovator*, represented by the foreigner. I also posit that this relationship is flexible enough to allow certain techniques of activation to be applied to the traditional legitimizing authority, *in its own social setting*, which can facilitate the acceptance and diffusion of the proposed innovation.

The need for a coordinated study and elaboration of such techniques – which I call techniques of micro-cooperation – is made urgent and compelling by the unprecedented increase in man's knowledge of his environment and his ability to control it. This aspect of the human intellect, because of its specific western technological approach and socio-economic motivations, is far from being equally distributed among men, and gives an unprecedented measure of control over the largest and weakest portion of humanity to that small fraction concentrated in the industrially developed states.

Micro-cooperation is not an independent system of aid-to-development. It is a claim for the integration into existing aid programmes of appropriate 'ignition' systems or circuits, to help start the engines of any development plan. In this sense, micro-cooperation is only one of the many tools available for international cooperation, and has no programmatic purpose of its own. It could, therefore, also be used to ignite engines which might, perhaps, be made to run in the wrong direction. Nor is the fact that developing countries might possess more experience in this type of aid-to-development than older and more developed countries, a guarantee that micro-cooperation techniques as employed by new states will serve better political purposes than the techniques of cooperation used by great powers. Micro-cooperation, however, does help small nations, even while still receiving aid for their own development, to participate effectively in the general process of international cooperation, and this is a positive factor in itself.

Turning to the dichotomy between the stranger and the foreigner, the dividing line between these carriers of innovation is not an easy one to draw, nor is it static. But the relationship between the carriers of innovation and the authority which legitimizes its diffusion, is a constant element from which we may draw one important generalization: the leadership of a society and the specific élite which legitimizes the introduction of an innovation, need not necessarily overlap. The 'Jean Laborde' model and the 'Eitan' model of micro-cooperation both show that, even in the most difficult and hostile situations, it is always possible to enrol the support of the traditional élite in favour of an innovation, provided that a coordinated effort is made (a) to separate the innovation from its foreign origin, and (b) to diffuse the innovation within its new context according to the logic of the people in the recipient society, and not according to that of the donor society.

Thus, if technical aid is regarded as a way of giving goods and ideas to the 'have nots' by the 'haves', then micro-cooperation is obviously an irrelevant approach, since it deals in men, and not in goods, or even ideas. If, however, by aid, we mean that type of help which the 'haves' extend to the 'have nots' in order to enable the latter to help themselves, then micro-cooperation, whatever its motivation, can make a difference to international cooperation and technical assistance.

It can do so both as a pragmatic technique of social engineering, and as a basic philosophical approach to the whole problem of sponsored development. Such an approach may not be very popular with people who believe in various types of determinism, and in maternal determinism in particular. It is, on the other hand, in line with the vision which social thinkers of the Age of Enlightenment had of man's development and of his capacity to learn from other men's experience. Micro-cooperation could be defined, according to the views of certain eighteenth-century philosophers, as a technique of aid-to-development based on the belief that mind 'is a highly combustible material which, however, does not ignite by itself'.[1]

Micro-cooperation is founded on the assumption that every society has its own virtues and that the best way to help people to develop is to help them to kindle their own 'internal vigour and virtue',[2] and not to help them acquire external vigour and alien virtues. This assumption may, of course, be dismissed as irrelevant by those who think that man is essentially a function of the institutions and environment in which he lives. For these people the most effective way to change human habits and attitudes will always be the manipulation of the environment and the institutions, and not the handling of the individuals.

The influence of environment and institutions on man's individual and collective behaviour should certainly not be underestimated. But there is no evidence to support the view that environmental change can develop a society more quickly and in a more controllable way than the proper activation of existing traditional élites in their own social setting. The contrary may well be true, and the costly failure of so many attempts at environmental and institutional change made by political régimes and by national and international aid agencies during the last ten years should make us suspect contemporary theories of economic and political development. Some of these theories can, at best, serve as guidelines for an *a posteriori* interpretation of an existing situation; never as guide-lines for people responsible for providing aid-to-development.

Micro-cooperation – that is, the coordinated effort of aid-to-development through the close cooperation of the men-in-the-middle and the members of the élites legitimizing the diffusion of their imported innovation – can be justified both by the accumulated experience of aid-advisers [3] in the field and by new theoretical approaches in the social sciences.[4]

Micro-cooperation directs its attention and efforts towards this inborn ability to create, which every socio-cultural structure possesses; the indigenous genius to innovate, which exists in every living society of men. As an approach to the problems of development, it holds that change and development cannot be brought about by the transfer – however well-intentioned or organized – of 'black boxes' of scientific, economic, religious or political innovation. It claims that it is only through the reaction elicited in men's minds by the way in which other men's views, techniques, products or behaviour are understood, that a meaningful dialogue of transculturation can be developed. If aid-to-development has to be effective, it must become a coordinated effort to promote such a dialogue among individuals, and to offer a body of techniques aimed to make the human dialogue about innovation easier and freer in spite of differences of culture and levels of development.

To claim more for micro-cooperation, would be preposterous. To claim less would be unfair to Leibnitz's admonition that 'nothing can be taught us of which we have not already in our mind an idea'.

A statement like that of the late President John F. Kennedy, that the United States could afford to give foreign aid and could

not afford not to give it, is thus a generous and self-enlightened
policy for the donor but certainly not a satisfactory policy for the
recipient. Foreign aid which is not able to promote self-help cannot really be regarded as aid-to-development. It still remains in
the category of charity, which is so frustrating because so often
it seems unending. To turn charity into aid, something else is
needed, namely the translation into practice of the consciousness
that every acquisition of a new technique, or any new use of an
old technique, regardless of its origin, alters man's social ecology.
To be acceptable, an innovation demands the restoration of a
balance between man and environment. Micro-cooperation may
not create new environments but it can, if properly handled, compensate for or help to repair the damage done by breaking an
established harmony – a break which often leads to the creation
of insurmountable opposition.

Appendix

West Bank

Table 1 **Population**

Period	Inhabitants (·000)
December 1967	595·9
December 1968	584·1
December 1969	599·6
December 1970	610·3
December 1971	623·6

Israeli Ministry of Defence, *Four Years of Military Administration 1967–1971*–1972, Page 15.

Table 2 **Agricultural Balance Sheet** (Current prices, IL millions)

	1968	1969	1970
The value of agricultural production	135	180	170
Purchased input	21	27	31
Resulting income	114	153	139

ibid., Page 22

Table 3   **Production** (in thousands of tons)

	1968	1969	1970
Wheat	18	33	23
Melons	36	21	13
Vegetables and potatoes	60	65	87
Olives	28	54	15

ibid., Page 23

Table 4   **The Value of Agricultural Output** (Current prices in IL millions)

	1968	1969	1970
Field crops	11	21	18
Melons	6	5	2
Vegetables and potatoes	20	23	27
Fruits	51	72	54
Afforestation of young plantations and others	2	3	3
Animals and animal products	45	56	65
Totals	135	180	169

ibid., Page 23

Table 5 **Per Capita Income**

Year	Per Capita G.N.P (I L)	Per Capita Gross (I L)	Per Capita Private Consumption (I L)
1965	—	802	—
1966	—	—	684
1967	—	—	—
1968	649	756	668
1969	788	852	782
1970	846	914	807

ibid., Page 17

(10·7 I L = 1 Pound Sterling)

Table 6 **Composition of Employment by Economic Sector (%)**

	1961	1969	1970
Agriculture	44	39	32
Industry	14	14	15
Construction	12	14	18
Services, trade and industry	30	33	35
Total	100	100	100

ibid., Page 20

Table 7 **Operating Budget**

	1969/70 Budget	Expenditure	1970/71 Budget	Expenditure
Prime Minister	268,000	267,939	299,000	299,000
Treasury	3,905,400	3,031,031	3,544,000	3,029,573
Health	5,742,200	6,405,688	6,539,000	8,002,072
Communications	2,833,000	2,665,965	2,506,000	2,550,126
Religions	745,000	570,717	334,000	224,830
Education	27,295,000	24,702,792	27,598,000	27,023,614
Agriculture	3,829,000	3,528,279	5,097,000	5,079,330
Trade and Industry	205,000	166,407	420,000	391,649
Police and Prisons	10,394,000	10,396,109	11,891,400	11,737,471
Justice	1,279,000	963,286	1,176,000	1,041,632
Welfare	3,964,000	3,216,795	3,600,000	3,437,729
Labour (including Public Works)	4,386,900	3,926,183	4,570,000	3,717,913
Interior	5,930,000	4,974,405	5,542,000	5,417,298
Government and Abandoned Property	1,039,000	747,264	929,000	717,117
Ministry of Development	—	—	56,000	32,088
Broadcasting Auth.	1,000,000	1,100,000	1,100,000	1,000,000
Housing	31,500	25,634	80,500	47,496
Transportation	1,121,500	746,130	1,223,000	751,576
Tourism	126,000	41,271	122,000	82,664
Civilian Admin.	1,495,000	1,003,937	1,250,000	1,063,854
Reserve	1,280,000	—	—	—
Total	76,869,500	68,479,832	77,876,900	75,647,032

Table 8 **Development Budget**

	1969/70 Budget	Expenditure	1970/71 Budget	Expenditure
Agriculture— afforestation	800,000	1,470,520	600,000	553,653
Water	2,943,000	1,232,336	3,783,000	2,900,720
Packing house	500,000	352,922	235,000	166,317
Roads and highways	6,050,000	7,334,462	6,620,000	6,866,107
Buildings	1,352,000	918,575	1,274,000	786,470
Development loans to local authorities	1,360,000	797,500	700,000	648,000
Credit fund for agriculture, transportation and industry	2,500,000	—	—	—
Water and agricultural surveys	1,810,000	872,090	1,642,000	1,561,976
School construction	1,500,000	248,467	—	—
Development of telephone lines	—	—	1,390,000	1,350,000
Loans from the credit fund	1,000,000	430,630	1,000,000	1,000,000
Income from repayment of loans	−1,000,000	−1,169,414	−1,000,000	−1,000,000
Bedouin settlement	—	—	300,000	21,750
Total Development	18,815,000	12,488,088	16,544,000	14,854,993
General Total	95,684,500	80,967,920	94,420,900	90,502,025

bid., Page 31

Notes

Chapter 1

1. Lester B. Pearson, *Partners in Development: Report of the Commission on International Development*, New York, 1969.
2. R. G. A. Jackson, *A Study of the Capacity of the United Nations Development System*. A report to the UNDP Administrator, Geneva, 1969.
3. *U.S. Foreign Assistance in the 1970's: A New Approach*. Report to the President from the Task Force on International Development, Washington, 1970.
4. Jan Tinbergen, Chairman, Committee for Development Planning. *Report on the Fourth and Fifth Session, ECOSOC*, New York, 1969.
5. *International Development Assistance*. A statement by the task force on international developmental assistance and international education of the National Association of State Universities and Land-Grant Colleges, Washington, 1969.
6. *The Rockefeller Report on the Americas*. Official report of a US Presidential mission for the Western Hemisphere, Chicago, 1969.
7. *Development Assistance in the New Administration*. A summary report of the President's General Advisory Committee on Foreign Assistance Programmes, October, 1968.
8. Pearson, op. cit., pp. 20–21.
9. ibid., p. 21.
10. Jay W. Forrester, *World Dynamics*, Cambridge, Mass., 1971.
11. Ruth Benedict, *Patterns of Culture*, London, 1945 (1935), p. 171.

Chapter 2

1. A. Hazlewood, *The Economics of Underdevelopment*, London, 1959, and Egbert de Vries, A Review of Literature on Development, *International Development Review*, Vol. 10, March 1969, pp. 43–52, are two different attempts in the field.
2. G. van der Veen, *Aiding Underdeveloped Countries through International Economic Cooperation*, Delft, 1954, pp. 18–61, gives a summary of the evolution of the concept of rights and duties of the states towards less advanced countries, from the 15th to the 20th century.
3. Gunnar Myrdal, *The Challenge of World Poverty: A World Anti-Poverty Program in Outline*, New York, 1970.
4. J. K. Galbraith, *The Underdeveloped Country*, Toronto, 1965.
5. M. Millikan and W. Rostow, *A Proposal: Key to Effective Foreign Policy*, New York, 1957.
6. US Senate, 1957, p. 20. Quoted by G. Ohlin, *The Evolution of Aid Doctrine: Foreign Aid Policies Reconsidered*, OECD, 1956, in J. Bhagwati and R. E. Eckhaus (eds.), *Foreign Aid*, London, 1970.
7. Gunnar Myrdal, *Challenge to Affluence*, New York, 1962–3, p. 128. For a survey of US contributions to European economic recovery see R. F. Minesell, *U.S. Economic Policy and International Relations*, New York, 1952, chap. 15.
8. J. R. Schlesinger, *The Political Economy of National Security*, New York, 1963, p. 63.
9. Jean-Jacques Servan-Schreiber, *The American Challenge*, trans. R. Steel, London, 1969.
10. Quoted by Eugene Staley (ed.), *Creating an Industrial Civilization*, A Report of the Coming Conference, London, 1952, p. 94.
11. G. Myrdal, *Development and Under-Development*, National Bank of Egypt, 50th Anniversary Commemoration Lecture, Cairo, 1956.
12. Milton Friedman, Foreign Economic Aid: Means and Objectives, *Yale Review*, Vol. 57, summer 1958, pp. 24–38.
13. ibid.
14. G. Ohlin, *The Evolution of Aid Doctrine: Foreign Aid Policies Reconsidered*, OECD, 1956; Z. Brzezinski (ed.), *Africa and the Communist World*, Stanford, 1965; David Morison, *The USSR and Africa – 1945–1963*, London, 1964; Elizabeth Kridl Valkener, New Trends in Soviet Relations with the Third World, *World Politics*, April, 1970.
15. J. Berliner, *Soviet Economic Aid*, New York, 1958.
16. Schlesinger, op. cit., p. 284.

17. OECD Statistics, quoted by Ohlin, in Bhagwati and Eckhaus, op. cit., p. 57.

18. ibid.

19. Tibor Mende, *Entre la Peur et l'Espoir, Réflexions sur l'Histoire d'Aujourd'hui*, Paris, 1958, pp. 33 ff.

20. ibid., p. 121.

21. A. Stevenson, *Call for Greatness*, New York, 1954.

22. Schlesinger, op. cit., p. 249.

23. Edward S. Mason, *Promoting Economic Development: The United States and Southern Asia*, Claremont, Cal., 1958.

24. J. K. Galbraith, 'It's Lucky Men Don't Control Events', reprinted in *Ceres*, Vol. 3, No. 2, March/April, 1970.

25. Y. Ye. Zhukov, 'The Bandung Conference of Asian and African Countries', *International Affairs*, No. 5, 1955, p. 32.

26. Morison, op. cit., p. 71.

27. K. Wittfogel, *Le Despotisme Orientale*, Paris, 1964. See also the later orthodox reinterpretation of the concept in: Maurice Godelier, 'La Notion de "Mode de Production Asiatique" et les Schemas Marxistes d'Évolution des Sociétés', in *Centre d'Études et des Recherches Marxistes Sur le 'Mode de Production Asiatique'*, Paris, 1969, pp. 48–100.

28. See Roger Garaudy's Preface to 'Sur le Mode de Production Asiatique' quoted in the previous note, which was written a short time before Garaudy himself was expelled from the French Communist Party.

29. Cyril A. Zabot, *The Economics of Competitive Coexistence: Convergence through Growth*, New York, 1964. Raymond Aron, *Eighteen Lectures on Industrial Society*, London, 1967.

30. Karl de Schweinitz, *Industrialisation and Democracy: Economic Necessities and Political Possibilities*, New York, 1964, quoted by M. Olson, Jr in: 'Some Social and Political Implications of Economic Development', *World Politics*, April, 1965, pp. 337–545.

31. Kurt Muller, 'Soviet and Chinese Programs of Economic and Technical Aid', in *The Soviet Bloc, China and Africa*, S. Hamrell and C. Gota Windstram (eds.), London, 1964, pp. 105–7.

32. J. K. Galbraith, *Economic Development in Perspective*, Harvard, 1962, pp. 12–14.

33. Friedman, op. cit.

34. It is beyond the purpose of this book to analyse the theories of economic development. See Bert E. Hoselitz, 'Balanced Growth, Destabilizers and the Big Push', *World Politics*, April, 1960, XII, No. 3, and Bert E. Hoselitz (ed.), *Theories of Economic Growth*,

New York, 1963; E. W. Singer, *International Development and Growth*, London, 1966; W. W. Rostow, *The Stages of Economic Growth*, Cambridge, Mass., 1969; Jose Medina Echavarrua and Benjamin Higgins, *Social Aspects of Economic Growth in Latin America*, UNESCO, Paris, 1953, ch. III; Paul Streefen, Unbalanced Growth, *Oxford Economic Papers*, New Series, Vol. I (1959), p. 157.

35. R. Nurkse, *Problems of Capital Formation in Underdeveloped Countries*, OUP, 1953, p. 70.

36. Notably that of B. E. Hoselitz, op. cit.

37. ibid., note 14.

38. UNO Economic Commission for Latin America, New York, 1950.

39. Dr L. Yablochkov, 'Socio-Demographic Disproportion of Africa in the Modern World', in Robert K. A. Gardiner, M. J. Anstee and C. L. Patterson (eds.), *Africa and the World*, Addis Ababa, 1970, pp. 245–8.

40. Gabriel A. Almond, *The Politics of the Developing Areas*, New York, 1960, and 'A Development Approach to Political System', *World Politics*, No. 9, January, 1965.

41. Samuel P. Huntington, Political Development and Political Decay, *World Politics*, April, 1965.

42. Samuel P. Huntington, *Political Order in Changing Societies*, Yale University Press, 1968, p. 8.

43. L. Mair, Social Changes in Africa, *International Affairs*, October 1960, p. 455.

44. Michael Polany, *The Logic of Liberty, Reflections and Rejoinders*, London, 1951, p. 21.

45. Ruth Benedict, op. cit., pp. 4–5.

46. ibid., p. 7.

47. Abram Kardiner, *The Individual and his Society: The Psychodynamics of Primitive Social Organization*, New York (1939) 1949, 5th printing, pp. 37 ff.

Chapter 3

1. For instance, C. R. Hensman, *Rich against the Poor: The Reality of Aid*, London, 1971, chap. IV. Or, for a new and more sophisticated treatment, Jay W. Forrester, *World Dynamics*, Cambridge, Mass., 1971, who suggests that the new development of underdeveloped areas may turn out to be one of the conditions for saving future global equilibrium.

2. J. B. Bury, *The Idea of Progress, an Inquiry into its Growth and Origin*, New York, 1955, Introduction p. xxiii.

3. Robert Delavignette, *Freedom and Authority in French West Africa*, OUP, London, 1950, translated from the French by the International African Institute Publications, p. 78.

4. Max Gluckman, *Political Law and Ritual in Tribal Society*, Oxford, 1965, p. 102.

5. Delavignette, op. cit., p. 75.

6. ibid., p. 77.

7. Gluckman, op. cit., pp. 14–15.

8. Delavignette, op. cit., p. 76. He notes that in Haussa country the canton chief is the *serky*, the landlord. The sultan of Haradi is called *Serky N'Fulani*. The generic name for village is *gari*, but the village chief is not called *Serky N'Gari* but *Mai-Gari*. A cameleer is the *Mai-Rakuni*; a horseman *Mai-Doki*; that is, a camelman, a horseman. Thus it appears that the *Mai-Gari* is not the lord of the village but the village-man, one with the village as the cameleer is one with the camel and the horseman one with the horse. The chief is one who symbolizes the village itself.

9. T. Kerstiens, *The New Élite in Asia and Africa*, New York, 1966.

10. ibid., p. 7.

11. Vilfredo Pareto, *The Mind and Society*, ed., Arthur Livingston, New York, 1935, quoted by Kerstiens, op. cit., p. 8.

12. Kersteins, op. cit., p. 8. On the role of the élites see what Kenneth E. Boulding has to say, in an entirely different context, in *The Image*, Michigan Press, 1956 (1961 edition), pp. 93, 107, and R. Weitz, *From Peasants to Farmers, A Revolutionary Strategy for Development*, New York, 1971, p. 71. Boulding discusses the dependence of human behaviour on the image man has of himself and his social role, and Weitz, the new orientation which he proposes for agricultural development.

13. Ronald Frankenberg, *The Handling of Conflict in Decision-Making Groups: The Village and the Nation*, Brit. Association Paper (mimeographed), Aberdeen, 1963.

14. Ronald Frankenberg, *A Village on the Border*, London, 1957, p. 44.
15. Gluckman, op. cit., p. 100.
16. ibid., p. 101.
17. Max Gluckman, in W. Allan and others, 'Land Holding and Land usage among the Plateau Tonga of Mazabuka District, a Reconnaissance Survey', *The Rhodes–Livingstone Papers*, No. 14, OUP, 1948, p. 181.
18. Alfred Schutz, *Collected Papers*, I, *Studies in Social Theory*, A. Brodensen (ed.), The Hague, 1964, 'The Stranger: an essay in Social Psychology', pp. 91–105.
19. ibid.
20. ibid.
21. ibid.
22. Kurt H. Wolff (ed. and translator), *The Sociology of Georg Simmel*, Part V, 'The Stranger', pp. 402–8.
23. *Recueils de la Société 'Jean Bodin'*, X, Brussels, 1958.
24. ibid., John Gilissen, 'Le Statut des Ètrangers à la Lumière de l'Histoire Contemporaine', pp. 5–57.
25. J. Ben-David, 'Roles and Innovation in Medicine', *The American Journal of Sociology*, Vol. LXV, No. 6, May, 1960, pp. 557–68.
26. Alfred Schutz, op. cit.
27. Peter Williams, Doc. 33, Philip Foster, *Education and Social Change in Ghana*, 1965, p. 177.
28. Peter Williams, 'Education for Development', *Conference on International Economic Development*, Columbia University, New York, 1970, p. 14.
29. C. E. Beeby, *The Quality of Education in Developing Countries*, OUP, 1966, chaps. IV and V.
30. The similarity which is often seen between the Weberian process of 'routinization of charisma' and the process of institutionalization of modernization, through 'charismatic' élites (S. E. Eisenstadt, *Modernization: Protest and Change*, Englewood Cliffs, N.J., 1966, p. 48) seems to be far more valid for underdeveloped countries than for developed ones, with the accent being put on the 'charismatic element' of the élite as much.

The distinction made by Paul Pigors in *Leadership or Domination*, Boston, 1935, between 'leadership' and 'headship' can usefully be borne in mind in this context, although it was originally meant to describe a different phenomenon. Cecil Gibb, 'Leadership: Psychological Aspects', *Encyclopedia of the Social Sciences*, p. 91.

Eisenstadt, op. cit., p. 9, sees in the growing dissociation between 'élite and broad status group', as well as among the different élites themselves, 'a very important aspect of the system of stratification that tended to develop with processes of modernization'.

31. The process by which the subject imitates the ruler, and the conquered adapt themselves to the conqueror was already observed by Ibn Khaldun in the fourteenth century. (*Prologomenae*, 1861, Vol. I, p. 306, Slane's translation.) It is a process which is creating many paradoxical reactions. Till very recently, it was held that any diffusion of imitation of the more developed over the less developed, be it through a spontaneous or compulsory process, meant also a diffusion of civilization (R. Maunier, *The Sociology of Colonies*, translated E. O. Lorrimer, London, 1949, p. 95). This 'colonialistic', even though well-intentioned, approach is now being challenged even in those fields in which colonization brought evident advantages to the colonies, such as relative prosperity, health and security. But, at the same time, this very same 'colonialistic' approach remains unchallenged in the fields of education and science. Indigenous leaders of newly independent countries often consider as an act of 'neo-colonialism' any attempt to make study curricula independent of metropolitan systems, even if the latter are clearly unfitted to local educational needs.

32. Some of the best modern African writers have made this problem the main theme of their novels. See, for instance, Chinua Achebe, *Things Fall Apart*, 1958, and Cheikh Hamidou Khane, *L'Aventure Ambiguë*, 1962.

33. A significant debate was held on the problem of the African intellectuals in Paris, and recorded in the mimeographed review of the Bureau d'Études des Réalités Africaines, December–January, 1964, No. 6. The African students in Paris saw that the pre-independence élites had worked for the philosophico-moral rehabilitation of the colonized man but not for his politico-social liberation because they had assimilated the culture of the colon. This culture, and particularly this language, which embodied the prestige values of the colonial administration, constituted the only terms of reference for promotion.

34. S. N. Eisenstadt, *The Protestant Ethic and Modernization*, New York, 1965, p. 3–45.

35. D. V. Segre, *Israel, a Society in Transition*, London, 1971, pp. 152–5.

Chapter 4

1. G. Ferrand, 'Les Voyages des Javanais à Madagascar', *Journal Asiatique*, 910, pp. 281–330, and Alfred and Guillaume Grandidier, *Collection des ouvrages concernant Madagascar* (1903–20), especially Vol. IX, Flacourt, 'Relation de la Grande Île de Madagascar' (1624–60); G. Grandidier, *Histoire politique et coloniale* (de Madagascar), 3 vols., Paris, 1958, Vols. I and II, 'Histoire des Merinas'; J. B. Razafintsalama, *La langue malgache et les origines malgaches*, 2 vols., Tananarive, 1928–9.

2. D. V. Segre, 'Madagascar: an example of indigenous modernization of a traditional society in the 19th century', *St Antony's Papers, No. 21: African Affairs*, OUP, 1969.

3. The most detailed report on the early stages of the tug-of-war between French adventurers, British missionaries and Malagasy politicians for the economic control of Madagascar, including the secret correspondence between Radama II and the French, is contained in Baron P. de Richemond, *Documents sur la Compagnie de Madagascar – Précédé d'une Notice Historique*, Paris, 1887. See also F. H. Bonnaboy de Premont, *Rapport a L'Empereur sur la question Malgache et la Colonisation de Madagascar*, Paris, 1850. For the later part of the negotiations concerning the attribution of economic rights to the French and the British at the time of Radama II, much relevant material, still unpublished, is contained in the dispatches of the first British Consul in Tananarive, J. B. Packenham, to the British Foreign Office: PRO, FO 48/9, 48/10, 1962, 1963.

4. For the full list of British missionaries and their families in Madagascar, from 1818–36, see: *Madagascar and its martyrs – a book for the Young, by the author of Missionary Stories, etc.*, London, 1852, pp. 18–19, and, *Register of LMS Missionaries*.

5. Born in Perthshire, Scotland, in 1800, he sailed for Madagascar in 1826 as an official carpenter of the Mission. His activities extended well beyond his job: he set up the first cotton mill in Madagascar at Amparibe, as well as the first printing press. It was mainly due to the desire of the Hova Government to keep him at the capital that permission for the continuation of missionary activities was granted from 1829–35. Cameron taught the Malagasy how to make soap, a manufacture which so much impressed them that it was probably a decisive element in obtaining permission for him to stay in the country. After leaving Madagascar in 1835, he established himself at Cape Town and returned

to Madagascar as a delegate of the Chamber of Commerce of Mauritius, to negotiate with the Malagasy Government for the renewal of trade with the Europeans, in 1853. After successfully completing his mission, he returned to the Cape, going back to Madagascar for the third time with Bishop Ellis in 1863, to supervise the erection of the Memorial Churches for the Martyrs of Madagascar. He died in Tananarive in 1875.

6. See W. N. Gunson, *Evangelical Missionaries in the South Seas, 1797-1860.*

7. The case of the transliteration of the Malagasy language is a famous and illuminating one. For several months the then head of the Mission in Tananarive, the Rev. David Jones, a Welshman, fought a bitter fight against the Rev. John Jeffreys, an Englishman, over the correct transliteration of the sound 'oo'. Jones wanted it represented by a 'w', while Jeffreys – a better educated man with a socially ambitious wife – insisted that the transliteration be made with a double 'o'. The fight, which was carried on with incredible ferocity, ended in a Court of Inquiry held by the British Agent, who had to investigate the reason for the Rev. Jeffreys having requested an audience with the King and having told him not to accept the Rev. Jones's suggestion, since this was based on the Rev. Jones's tribal attachment to a low caste British tribe who use 'a mean language, which is Welsh'. The King, who was quick to discern the personal and social animosity underlying the quarrel, finally fixed the transliteration by a decree, ordering that some of the vowels and diphthongs be transliterated according to French grammar and others according to English. LMS Box 1, Folder 4, Jeffreys to Jones, 1 April 1823, and Jones and Griffiths to, 24 April 1823.

8. The case of the Rev. W. Griffith is a typical one. He amassed a considerable fortune in Tananarive, becoming one of the main money-lenders in the capital, a situation which he did not wish to abandon when recalled to England by the Directors of the LMS. His relations with other members of the Mission were so bad that he involuntarily became instrumental in supplying the Malagasy with many of the accusations which were later used to justify the expulsion of the missionaries from the country. He was probably also instrumental in worsening the relations of the British Agent, Dr Lyall, with the Malagasy authorities. LMS Archives, Madagascar, Box 3, Folder 1, Minutes of the Meeting of the Mission Members, 2 February 1829, and LMS Archives, Madagascar,

Cameron to Arundel, Box 4, Folder 2, 11 April 1832; Johns to Arundel, 15 April 1832.

9. Lyall to Jones, LMS Archives, Madagascar, Box 3, Folder 1, 13 August 1828.

10. *Le Journal de Robert Lyall*, translated by G.-S. Chapus and G. Mondain, Académie Malgache, Vol. V, 1954, Lyall's entry of 2 February 1829, p. 170.

11. The missionaries were naturally a very important source of political information for the British Government, and in some cases the only available translators of official documents and conversations. Some of the reports they were asked to send back to the LMS in London were, in fact, detailed answers to political questionnaires. See, for instance, the unsigned questionnaires on Malagasy politics and religion, probably dated the end of 1832, LMS Archives, Madagascar, Box 4, Folder 1. In some instances the missionaries far exceeded their religious role. This seems to have been the case with the Rev. Freeman, a leading member of the Tananarive Mission, who apparently had no small share in the responsibility for the failure of the Malagasy diplomatic mission sent by the Queen to London in 1836–7 to re-establish relations with the British Government without restoring missionary activities. See: Freeman to Palmerston, 4 February 1837, 23 February 1837, 18 March 1837, PRO, FO 48/1. It is also interesting to note that although there are abundant proofs in the Foreign Office correspondence of the time of the initiative taken by the Rev. Freeman in connection with the Malagasy missions, no trace of this correspondence can be found in the archives of the LMS itself.

12. As I have said above, it is not impossible that many of the accusations made by the Malagasy against the British Agent, Dr Lyall, were – at least in part – suggested to the Malagasy by the Rev. Griffith himself. See: David Jones to W. Orme, Foreign Secretary, LMS, from Port Lewis, Mauritius, 16 September 1830, Box 3, Folder 4.

13. The missionaries' idea was to establish a Society for the Advancement of Education among the Malagasy which would draw its income directly from patrons in England and thus add to the income of the Mission, as the money would be over and above the sum the Mission was receiving from LMS headquarters in London. The King agreed in the first instance to be the President of the Society and also agreed that some of his Generals should join as well. He became very cool, however, when he learned that the Society's decisions would be taken by the Board on the basis of a

majority vote. 'For a proposition to be carried out by a majority in a Society in which he [the King] belonged would not do in this country, where the word of the King is law.' Jones and Griffith to Burder, LMS Archives, Madagascar, Box 2, Folder 2, 19 December 1825.

14. This is somewhat different from what happened in other non-European countries, where western techniques were far more appreciated than the metaphysical and cultural framework which produced them. This may be due to the deep religious character of the Malagasy society. A modern analysis of their religious attitudes which throws much interesting light on the reaction of the Malagasy to the European spiritual impact, has been written by a religious scholar in Tananarive, the Rev. Richard Andriamanjato, *Le Tsiny et le Tody*, Tananarive, 1957. The author, who is a leading Marxist political figure in Madagascar, is significant also as a descendant of the first Christian aristocratic families of Madagascar, who were involved in the modernization of the country in the eighteenth century.

15. An idea of what the Malagasy thought of the missionaries as a political force can be obtained from the report sent by Johns to Arundel, LMS Archives, Madagascar, Box 4, Folder 2, 15 April 1832.

16. Freeman to Hunkey, LMS Archives, Madagascar, Box 4, Folder 2, 10 June 1832, about the behaviour of three of the Malagasy trainees who had returned from England. The behaviour of the European-trained Malagasy intellectuals of those days seems to me to be an early example of the behaviour of many contemporary native intellectuals, who are supposed to assist the European advisers in their work of transculturation, but cannot overcome their complexes. The frustrated assistant technical advisers, the over-confident, emotionally unsatisfied Peace Corpsmen, the reticent native officials parachuted into jobs for which they are not prepared and for which they do not wish to be responsible – all seem to reflect the state of mind, the inhibitions, the self-destructive and pessimistic approach which appears in the 'men-in-the-middle' of old Madagascar.

17. Until the British Agent was expelled, Brady, already a General in the Malagasy army received his sergeant's pay from the British paymaster in Mauritius, despite the fact that he was no longer a serving soldier and had taken up Malagasy citizenship.

18. The complicated personal relations between Hastie and his superiors in Mauritius are well illustrated by the tone of the cor-

respondence he conducted with the British Governor, Sir Robert Farquhar, and the Acting-Governor, General Gage Hall. With the former, a civilian who had a keen appreciation of Hastie's qualities and did not hesitate to appoint him British Agent in Tananarive despite his sergeant's rank, Hastie exchanged deferent but very cordial letters. See, for example, Hastie to Farquhar, 3 June 1818, PRO, CO 167 51. On the other hand, the very fact that Hastie was a sergeant was sufficient reason for General Hall, a rigid disciplinarian, to describe him as a second-rate person and not to take his political advice into consideration. Hall to Bathurst, 26 June 1818, PRO, CO 163 39.

19. Raombana manuscript, op. cit., Vol. II, p. 95.

20. The accusations and counter-accusations between the missionaries and the British Agent are contained in the reports of a court of inquiry set up to investigate the charges of Dr Lyall against Griffith, which also give a summary of the correspondence exchanged between the Agency and the Mission during the period 1 February 1831 and 2 November 1831. LMS Archives, Madagascar, Box 4, Folder 3.

21. *Le Journal de Robert Lyall*, op. cit., entry of 2 February 1829, p. 171.

22. Fontoynont and Nicol, *Memoires de l'Académie Malgache*, Vol. XXXIII, Tananarive, 1940.

23. Pakenham to Earl Russell, 1 December 1862, PRO, FO 48 9.

24. Robert E. Park in the introduction to *The Marginal Man – a Study in Personal and Cultural Conflict*, by Everett V. Stonequist, New York, 1961, p. 18. The problem of the marginal man is discussed by H. F. Dickie-Clark, *The Marginal Situation, A Sociological Study of a Coloured Group*, New York, 1959, chapter 1 – 'The Theory of the Marginal Man and its Critics', pp. 7–25. This book, however, refers mainly to the marginality of the man who belongs to a lower status or minority group. We, however, are interested in the marginality which is connected with power and authority, as defined in Carl J. Friedrich's terms, namely that power seems to be 'that relation among men which manifests itself in the behaviour of following'. 'Political leadership and the power of charismatic power', *Journal of Politics*, Vol. 23, 1961, p. 5.

25. See Stonequist, op. cit., chapters 2, 3 and 4, dealing with the racial and cultural hybrid, a well as Joseph Ben-David on the role of the social hybrid in scientific discovery, *Minerva*, Vol. IV, No. 1, Autumn, 1965.

26. The preliminary results of a study carried out on the motivation

of Israeli technical assistance operators overseas, between the years 1958 and 1968, show that there is no apparent relationship between the feeling of social marginality of the operators themselves and their success or otherwise in their work as vehicles of transculturation. I am grateful for this information which I received from Dr Naomi Hazan, who is working on problems of African modernization as a part of her doctoral thesis at the Hebrew University.

27. E. V. Stonequist, op. cit., p. 221.

28. Kurt H. Wolff (ed.), op. cit., pp. 402–8, G. Simmel, 'The Stranger'.

29. I am grateful to Professor Robert Merton for suggesting this description of the man who stands between two cultures, and also for the many helpful suggestions he generously gave me for the correction of this part of my paper.

30. Pierre Boiteau, *Madagascar: contribution a l'histoire de la nation malgache*, Paris, 1958.

31. Raombana manuscript, op. cit., Vol. II, pp. 107, 108 ff.

32. ibid.

33. P. de la Vaissière, *Histoire de Madagascar, ses habitants et ses missionaires*, Paris, 1882, 2 vols.

34. It is interesting to note that one of the claims made by the French to justify the occupation of Madagascar was the dispute over the estate of Jean Laborde, the very man who, more than any other European, contributed to the modernization of Madagascar and who himself had become a Malagasy citizen of high standing. Deschamps, op. cit., pp. 182, 186.

35. See: *Peace Corps Bibliography, March 1961–March 1965*, Division of Public Information, Peace Corps, Washington, 1965; the *Peace Corps Reader*, Office of Public Affairs, Peace Corps, Washington, 1969; David Hapgood, *Agents of Change, A Close Look at the Peace Corps*, Boston, 1968; and Brent Ashabranner, *A Moment of History: The First Ten Years of the Peace Corps*, New York, 1971.

36. Robert B. Textor (ed.), *Cultural Frontiers of the Peace Corps*, MIT Press, 1966, p. 37.

37. ibid., Preface, p. xiii.

38. ibid., pp. 233 ff.

39. ibid., p. 107.

40. ibid., p. 122.

41. W. B. Heath, 'The Emerging Volunteer Subculture in Bolivia', in Textor, op. cit., p. 271.

42. ibid., p. 278.
43. ibid., p. 279.
44. Textor, op. cit., p. 37.
45. ibid., p. 5.
46. ibid., p. 311.
47. ibid., p. 317.

Chapter 5

1. Leopold Laufer, *Israel and the Developing Countries: New Approaches to Cooperation*, New York, 1967, pp. 65–8.
2. The *Moshav* (settlement) is a cooperative settlement, with each family organizing its own private life, but linked with the others through common ownership of land and means of production, and by the common marketing of products. Stress is laid on the élitist element and on ideological identity. Immigrants from Germany in the late 1930s evolved a mixture of *Kibbutz* (collective settlement) and *Moshav*, callel *Moshav Shitufi*, in which the community's ideological control over its members was greater than in the *Moshav*; the economy and ownership were collective as in the *Kibbutz*, but each family had its own house and was responsible for its own cooking, laundry and care of children, as in the *Moshav*, while work and pay were adjusted to individual circumstances. In addition the *Moshav Shitufi*, like the *Kibbutz*, tends to develop industry as well as agriculture.
3. Albert Meister, *Principes et Tendences de la Planification Rurale en Israel*, Paris, 1962; H. Darin-Drabkin, *Planification Rurale en Israel, un Aspect Régional*, Jerusalem, 1960 (roneoed); H. Halperin, *Changing Patterns in Israel Agriculture*, London, 1957, and *Agrindus*, Paris, 1966; Ministry of Agriculture, *Background Data on the Lachish Region*. R. Weitz, *From Peasants to Farmers, A Revolutionary Strategy for Development*, New York, 1971, gives many examples of the application of the agricultural development methods developed in Israel and a useful selected bibliography on the subject.
4. Frank Michael, *Cooperative Land Settlements in Israel and their Relevance to African Countries*, Basle, 1968.
5. Maxwell I. Klayman, *The Moshav in Israel, A Case Study of Institution Building for Agricultural Development*, New York, 1970, chapter 10; R. Weitz and A. Rokach, *Agricultural Development, Planning and Implementation*, (Israel Case Study), Dordrecht, 1968.
6. J. K. Galbraith, 'Underdevelopment – An Approach to Classification', in *Fiscal and Monetary Problems in Developing Countries*, D. Krivine (ed.), New York, 1967.
7. Ministry of Agriculture Center for Agricultural Cooperation with Developing Countries, The El-Sisal Development Project, Azva Province, Dominican Republic, a joint OEA-Israel-BID Project, *A Synopsis of the Rural Development Plan*, Rehovot, Israel, December 1970.

8. For a summary of Israel's cooperation activities in Latin America see: División de Cooperación Internacional, Ministerio de Relaciones Exteriores, *Sumario de los Programas de Cooperación nacional en las Americas*, Jerusalem, 1971. See also R. Weitz, op. cit. (n. 3) pp. 107, 109, for a brief description of the Israeli development scheme in Venezuela.

9. Ministry of Agriculture, Center for Agricultural Cooperation with Developing Countries, The Planning of a Regional Area (6000 hectares) in the Vientiane Plain Project, a joint Laotian–Israel Project, *A Synopsis of the Rural Development Plan*, Rehovot, Israel, January 1971.

10. Ministry for Foreign Affairs, Division for International Cooperation, *Proposed Israeli Cooperation in Agricultural and Water Development in the Kingdom of Nepal*, Jerusalem, 1961.

11. Republic of Zambia, Ministry of Rural Development, Department of Cooperative Societies, *The Kafulafuta and Kafubu Cooperative Settlement Projects*, Vol. I, 'Planning Approach and Agricultural Plan', The Center for Agricultural Cooperation with Developing Countries, Rehovot, Israel, April 1970.

12. Letter dated 5 May 1969, from the Secretary of the Israeli *Moshav* (Cooperative) Movement to Eitan Israely. Personal Interview.

13. For a lively description of the situation on the West Bank of the Jordan after the Six-Day War, and of the Israeli policy in the occupied areas, see Shabtai Tevet, *The Cursed Blessing*, London, 1969.

14. This improvised solution has since become the policy of 'open bridges' which is still in force, with hundreds of thousands of Arabs crossing the Jordan every year, from both sides of the river.

15. The fact that the two original marketing cooperatives (one in the Hebron district, the other in Samaria) and the olive oil processing and marketing cooperative established by the Jordanians continued to operate after the short break due to the fighting and resumed the export of agricultural production east of the Jordan, acted as an important stimulus for farmers to organize themselves for the purpose of exporting their products to Jordan, in spite of the new political situation.

16. The occupied areas' total imports in 1970 were IL 295 million, as against IL 263 million in 1968. The Israeli share had grown from IL 179 million to IL 252 million (i.e. from 25 per cent to 86 per cent) while the Jordanian share dropped from 8 per cent to 4 per cent. With regard to exports from the occupied areas, these rose from about IL 137 million in 1969 to IL 146 million in 1970, of

which Israel bought 34 per cent in 1969 and 41 per cent in 1970. The Jordanian share declined, from IL 69 million (50 per cent) to IL 60 million (41 per cent). See: Ministry of Agriculture Command of Judea and Samaria regions, *Summary of Activities During Three Years in the Agriculture of Judea and Samaria*, April 1970, mimeographed in Hebrew.

17. Brigadier-General Shlomo Gazit, Rehovot Seminar, 21 April 1969.

Conclusion

1. August Wilhelm von Schlegel, 'De l'étymologie en général', in E. Böcking (ed.), *Oevres écrites en Français*, Leipzig, 1846, p. 127.
2. J. Harris, *Works*, Earl of Malmesbury (ed.), London, 1901, p. 209; quoted by N. Chomsky in *Cartesian Linguistics: a chapter of rationalist thought*, New York, 1966, note 115.
3. Dudley Seers, 'Why Visiting Economists Fail', *The Journal of Political Economy*, Vol. LXX, August 1962, No. 4, pp. 325–38.
4. This is very much in accordance with the ideas developed by R. Weitz, *From Peasants to Farmers, A Revolutionary Strategy for Development*, ch. 17, in which he deals with 'activators and activated'.

Index

acculturation, 47, 80
Afghanistan, 69–70, 92–8, 144
Africa, 104; agriculture in, 5, 106, 113–15; colonial rule in, 61–2; and communism, 24–6, 28; educational problems in, 58; modernization in, 41, 51; the 'stranger' in, 50–51; traditional chiefs in, 41–3, 45
Africanization, 37
agriculture, 4–5, 65, 100–143
Allensi clan, 51
Almond, G. A., 34
American Peace Corps, 70, 85–100
Amman, 110, 112, 119, 122–4
Arab Agricultural Cooperatives, 125
Arab agriculture (after 1967 war), 100–143
Arab–Israeli War (1967), 100–101, 110, 114, 125, 140
Arabs, Palestinian, 63–4
Asia, 104, 106; and Marxism, 25
Aswan Dam, 4
Axis powers, 14

Bandung Conference (1955), 24, 27–8, 33
BBC, 32
Bedouin, 110
Ben Herut, Ze'ev, 117
Benedict, Ruth, 6
Berliner, Joseph, 18
Bolivia, 98
Bourbon (La Réunion), 70
Brady, 77
Brazil, 4–5
Bridge over the River Kwai, The, 143
B'sor, 103
Buganda, 61

California University, 120
Cameron, James, 72
China, 18–19, 21, 24, 28, 32, 70, 76, 111
Chou En-Lai, 24, 28
Cold War, 8, 14, 18, 21, 28, 33
colonial rule, 61–2
colonialism, 17–18
Common Market, 10
communism, 14, 21–6
communist aid, 17–21

communist societies, 60
Cornell University, 87, 89–90

Dahomey, 4, 105
Dayan, General Moshe, 64,
    108–10
Delavignette, Robert, 42–3
dollar gap, 14–15
Dominican Republic, 106
Doughty, Professor Paul L.,
    88–9, 91
Dupree, Louis, 92–3, 95–6

education, 5, 58–9, 62–3
Egypt, 5, 29; Military
    Administration in Gaza,
    108–9
Eisenstadt, S. N., 64
El-Sisal Development Project,
    106
'elite', in society, 47–9, 55,
    60–64, 94, 98–9, 104, 144,
    147; in Madagascar, 72,
    75–7, 85; in Peru, 92;
    in Jordan, West Bank, 138
Europeanization, 36–7
Evans-Pritchard, E. E., 32

FAO, 4–5
Farquhar, Sir Robert, 70
'foreigners' in society, 53–60,
    65, 83–4, 102, 140, 143
Frankenberg, Ronald, 50
Fraser, Sir James, 32
Friedman, Milton, 16–17, 23,
    29–30, 33

Gabon, 49
Galbraith, John Kenneth,
    10–11, 23, 26, 68, 104–6
de Gaulle, Charles, 15
Gaza strip, 108

Gefen, David, 117
Geneva Convention, 108
Givati, Haim, 123
Gluckman, Max, 43, 51
Goldstein, Avraham, 117
Greece, 12
Greeks (ancient), 54–5
Grotius, 9

Hailey, Lord, 28
Hannah Report, 2
Hastie, James, 77–8, 81, 93
Heath, W. B., 98
Hebron, 110, 122
Huntington, Professor, 32,
    34–5

India, 41, 76, 106
Indiana University, 88
Iraq, 5
Israel, 6, 28, 32; aid to
    underdeveloped countries,
    102–7; immigrants in, 102–5
Israeli Army, 108, 110, 114
Israeli occupation of Jordan,
    West Bank, 59, 100, 108–43
Israely, Eitan, 114–18, 127–8,
    131, 142, 145
Italy, 41
Ivory Coast, 42, 118

Jackson Report, 2, 10–11, 39
Japan, 41, 70, 76
Jean Bodin Society, 54
Jerusalem, 110–11, 122, 127
Jerusalem Post, The, 125
Jerusalem University, 114
*Jewish Observer and Middle
    East Review, The*, 120
Jews, 49; in Mandatory
    Palestine, 63–4

Jordan: British tradition in, 63–4; occupied by Israelis, 108
Jordan, West Bank, 110–28, 131–42, 143
Judea, Southern, 110
Jura, 'depressed zones' of, 10

Kabul, 93–4
Kardiner, Abram, 38
Kariba Dam, 4
Katzir, Yaakov, 117–18
Kennedy, President John F., 86, 147
Kenya, 61
Kenyatta, Jomo, 51
Kerstiens, Thom, 47
kibbutz, 105, 107, 118, 124
Kuan Tzu, 46
Kuwait, 13, 133–4

Laborde, Jean Baptiste, 71, 79–81, 145
Lachish, 103, 118
Laos, 106
Latin America, 5, 104, 106; and Marxism, 25
Leibnitz, 145
Lend-Lease Act, 14
Lenin, Leninism, 25, 32
de Lestelle, M., 79
L'Express, 15
Lindemann-Tozard controversy, 50
Lyall, Dr Robert, 78

macro-cooperation, 46
Madagascar, Malagasy society, 37, 56, 67, 69–85, 90–91, 93–5, 98–9, 144
Mair, Lucy, 35
Malenkov, 24

Marshall Plan, 13–14, 100
Marx, Marxism, 8, 16–18, 20, 24–6, 34, 76, 105
Mason, Edward S., 23
Mauritius, 70, 77
Melanesia, 37
Mesopotamia, 84
micro-cooperation, 45–8, 59–60, 66, 102, 143–6
Middle East agriculture, 5
'middle-men', in society, 49–52, 55, 57, 59–60, 65, 144
Millikan, M., 13
missionaries, 54; in Madagascar, 72–7, 84–5, 90–91, 94
MIT, 13, 16–17
Morison, David, 24
Moshav system, 103–6, 114, 117
Moslems, 93
Myrdal, Gunnar, 10–11, 16

Nablus, 110, 122, 124
Nadel, 47
Nasser, 28
Nehru, 28
Nepal, 106
New York slums, 10
Nigeria, 34, 61, 105
Nurske, 30

Pakistan, 93, 106
Palestine, 34, 63–4, 122
Palestine nationalism, 110
Pan, Mrs Ramma, 15
Pareto, Vilfredo, 47–8
Park, Robert E., 80
Pearson Report, 1–3, 9–10, 58
Perkins Report, 2
Peru, 69–70, 87–92, 97, 106, 144
Peterson Report, 2
Polynesia, 37
pragmatism, 102–3, 105

Prebish, Professor Raoul, 31
Pruginin, Yoel, 117
Puno Scheme (Peru), 106

Radama II, 71
Radama I, 71
Radcliff-Brown, Professor, 32
Rafman, Amos, 117
Ranavalona I, 71
Robin, 78
Rockefeller Report, 2
Rostow, W., 13
Rothschilds, 50
Rothwell, Easton, 47

Samaria, 110, 114, 117
Scandinavian countries, 12
Schlesinger, J. R., 15
Schutz, Alfred, 56, 84
de Schweinitz, Karl, 26
Schweitzer, Dr Albert, 49
Senegal, 61, 105
Servan-Schreiber, J.-J., 15
Shook, Cleo, 92–3
Sicily, 10
Simmel, Georg, 53, 56–7, 81–4,
    142
Sinai Campaign (1956), 108
Sino-Soviet bloc, 17–19
Snow, C. P., 50
'strangers' in society, 52–7, 59,
    65, 83–4, 102, 142, 145
Sudan, 24
Sukarno, 28
Sweden, 12
Syria, 13

technology, 40, 43–5
Tevet, S., 101
Textor, Robert, B., 99–100
Third World, 15–16, 24–5, 28,
    103
Tinbergen Report, 2
transculturation, 47, 52, 60, 64–5,
    72, 81–2, 144
Turkey, 12

Uganda, 42
'Ugly American' concept, 24, 86,
    87
Ugly American, The, 68
Ugly Russian, The, 68
UN agencies, 10–11, 39. *See also*
    FAO, UNESCO, WHO
UN Charter, 9
UNESCO, 4
USA: American aid, 12–13,
    15–17, 30; and communism,
    21–2. *See also* American
    Peace Corps
USSR, 18–19, 24, 28, 93

Vietnam, 12, 46, 109
Vitoria, 9

Webster, 83
WHO, 4
Williams, Peter, 59
Wittfogel, Karl, 25

Zambia, 106